Reflections of a Workaholic

Reflections of a Workaholic

Lessons on Life and Leadership from a
Twenty Year Corporate Executive

By

Jim McKay

REFLECTIONS OF A WORKAHOLIC

For more information please contact The Avleca Group Inc. at www.avleca.com or info@avleca.com

ISBN-13: 978-1540470232
ISBN-10: 1540470237

For my girls.

May you continue to demonstrate
strength, courage and conviction
in all you do.

Acknowledgements

This book was over twenty years in the making, with several players, participants and mentors shaping who I am as a leader.

Special thanks go to Bob and Chris – you have both shaped my career, leadership style and success with your wisdom, guidance and tireless belief in my abilities.

Thank you for being there when we needed you most…

Introduction

Staring at the ceiling. That is how the concept of what you are about to read came to be. I have spent the better part of over twenty years perfecting the art of multi-tasking - cramming in one more note, one more call and one more project. Ironic that it was a moment 'reflecting' that drove me to start penning stories of my corporate and life experiences into the works you are about to explore.

Why the sudden desire to tell these stories? In large part, my decision to venture into business for myself was a big part of it. To drive my new company, I would have to revisit some of the key skills and traits that drove my corporate success. Not only would I have to leverage my twenty years of leadership and driving change, but I would also have to build a client base and book of business from scratch in today's competitive landscape.

I've spent the last few months reflecting on my corporate career and building my new company. Strange to be in two concurrent places but not uncomfortable, given my efforts and hard work are all building towards my brand and company, not a bunch of shareholders I may never meet or even be relevant to. There is a certain rush that comes from building and driving a successful business – what you build is yours, and what you become as a brand and company is whatever you aspire it to be.

As someone who consistently relishes in the next meeting, negotiation, project or business opportunity, the thought of taking time for my own business was a distant daydream a year earlier. The ambition was always there, but the determination and push to actually go and do it was always just out of reach.

I've come to accept and appreciate the curse of the workaholic. In the corporate world, this acted as a virtuous circle for me and many others I have worked with over the years;

- Crush through one more meeting / email / call after the time you committed to leave
- Convince yourself to work more at night so you can get home to see your kids before bedtime
- Leave a little earlier in the morning so you can hit the gym on your way into the office
- Bring the laptop and phone to the rink or ball diamond to 'catch up'.

While most if not all of these are now common events for the average employee, reflecting on my twenty years of practicing these habits have rendered me quite capable of finding time to work all the time. What I have also realized is it is much more rewarding when you are doing so for the benefit of your client <u>and</u> your own company.

In the pages that follow, I will be sharing some of the events and opportunities that have shaped my character, leadership style and personal values. I'm penning this series of reflections not only as a retrospective look back for a set of advice I would give to my twenty-year-old self, but also as a toolbox for other up and coming executives and ambitious leaders young and old to consider what makes a successful leader. I hope you enjoy the read and hope it helps you in your journey from where you are today to where you are heading, be it in the corporate world or as an entrepreneur.

About the Author

Jim McKay is a trusted advisor, writer, father and seasoned supply chain executive with deep roots in the retail and industrial gas sectors.

In January, 2016 he founded The Avleca Group, a boutique consulting firm based in the Greater Toronto Area of Ontario, Canada.

Jim helps corporate clients develop an end to end strategy blueprint that drives world class culture and engagement, connecting the dots from the shop floor to the board room.

He is sought out for not only his ability to drive improvement in all sizes of business, but also to serve as trusted advisor to executives and key leaders as they embark on transformational change initiatives.

Jim holds an undergraduate degree from the University of Western Ontario, an Executive MBA from the Smith School of Business at Queen's University, is a Six Sigma Blackbelt, a Chartered Public Accountant (CPA, CMA) and holds the CCLP (Certified CITT Logistics Professional) designation.

For more information on Jim and his company please visit
www.avleca.com

Contents

<u>1</u>

"Share the Podium"

The Bigwheel Story

When I was a kid in the late 1970's I had one of the best toys ever invented (personal bias) – a "Bigwheel". I rode it so often the hard plastic wheels wore right down. Perhaps the part that was most entertaining about the Bigwheel was the races we would have on the street. The local kids would all gather, ride and race on the sidewalk and compete for pride and bragging rights. I still remember having the victory ceremonies complete with pretend podium and shaking up a coke bottle for the 'champagne' celebration. Through that experience among others, the concept of winning and losing was instilled in me very early. All through grade school, we did not have 'participation' ribbons like they do for kids today; it was a win-lose scenario in almost all sporting seasons, events and in particular – the Bigwheel races on the street.

Fast forward to today and much is the same in business. Companies win and lose every day. The proverbial 'podium' is chased via sales, profitability, market share, and brand perception for companies, along with ratings, likes, and retweets in the social media space. While not much has changed in the world as it relates to winners / losers, there has certainly been a great deal of evolution in terms of how one arrives at that destination. Namely, the requirement to involve other avenues, players and approaches has certainly transformed winning to a team game. Winning in business is now more than ever a team game, with the stakes seemingly higher every day.

In the Canadian business landscape, there are many examples of iconic brands that have disappeared, some seemingly overnight. From coast to coast and across industry, there are companies that seemed to have everything going for them only to have it go painfully wrong for shareholders, employees and customers alike. Much has been written about iconic corporations and their ungraceful exit from the Canadian business scene. What appears more obvious now than ever is the tightrope that many firms are walking in this win / lose environment. Forgiveness is rare, and results can trump common sense in many instances.

From my own leadership experience, the key to success is to leverage your team members, associates, vendors and customers to help you win – together. This holds true more now than it did when I first set foot in the corporate world. Though not less important then, it seemed the stakes were not as high as they are today, nor the implications so severe. There are two examples that come to mind that I would share with my twenty-year-old self if I was starting out all over again, both of which follow.

The Winning Bid

In the chemicals business, the lead times and business cycle for getting awarded new business can be very long – years in fact. The ability to pedal faster by yourself as if you're on the Bigwheel and ride to victory does not apply in this case. Rather, there is a need to pool together the right resources, expertise and references to get your business proposal across the line. This 'pit crew' type approach may not be entirely visible to the end customer, but can be called upon during the process to provide knowledge, validation and connectivity at the right time to drive your proposal forward. When done in a timely and precise manner, your very small local team of 2-3 resources can quickly swell to 20-30 at the right time to ensure you have the right expertise in the room at the right time to instill confidence in your approach, proposal and ultimately your organization.

In many large companies, associates can be left to feel they are alone in their quest to capture the sale, finish the project, and deliver the numbers. Such is not the case. Like most opportunities you will encounter in life, you are going to be much more successful and likely to accomplish your goals if you empower and involve others around you in a common cause. Rally your pit crew and drive your results faster and with more precision.

The Business Process

During my time in retail - both as a young adult working in produce and more recently as a Supply Chain executive, I learned that inventory efficiency can be a key driver of success for business. While the concept of 'reducing' inventory sounds simple, the process by which one goes about it involves many more steps and resources than I would have surmised going in. In a very recent example, we were tasked with reducing a significant amount of inventory from the network over a three-year period. We accomplished the goal, but not by traditional brute-force pedalling down the street.

In the end, success was delivered through multiple channels and processes including but not limited to: building a measurement system to define productive vs. non-productive inventory, creating rules to define promotions and product life cycles, building a reverse logistics channel to remove end of life product from stores, driving in store process to empty backrooms and implementing internal financial penalties for non-conformance to business process. Put simply, the processes and programs laid out to achieve success required cross functional alignment and execution from all corners of the business, something I would not have foreseen going into the program. In the end, we achieved an outcome even greater than our lofty expectations, and the podium needed to celebrate success was actually a stage.

Takeaways

The message in all of this I would convey to my 20-year-old self is the celebration of success as a team. Individual performance will always be important, measured and incented accordingly. That said, the power of working and celebrating success together as a team will almost always outweigh what you can accomplish on your own. Sharing the podium with your pit crew will continue to set you and your organization up for success for your current and future projects.

<u>2</u>

"Listen"

The Phone Story

I've read a lot of discussions lately about people's attention spans decreasing and the ability to listen to others fully all but disappearing. There is no question that the rapid advance of technology and the infinite stream of information has changed the way people think, behave and conduct themselves. Take a look around you in any public setting and see for yourself how many people simply cannot put their devices down, even when engaged in a conversation or key life moment. Our incessant desire to stay connected to email, social media, sports scores and the latest news and entertainment info has in many ways replaced good old conversation and connection. The downside of this is the numbing of our listening capabilities and more importantly, our ability to truly understand and be present in our work, home and social environments.

Having been caught up in the wave of technology myself, I think the access to information and constant barrage of emails and updates available to us has can have quite a drastic impact on one's ability to have a genuine conversation where there is a common understanding and connection. Reflecting back on my own career, I see many parallels to the commentary bantered around today about active listenting. When I first left University in the mid 1990's and entered the workforce, I felt like I had all of the answers. Fresh out of school and armed with knowledge, vigour and a ready-for-the-world approach, I set out to make my mark early on and get my career off to a running start. I excitedly accepted my first device - a Blackberry, not knowing that this would be the first step in my embracing the twenty-four-hour workday.

Sure, your employer doesn't expect you to work all day and all night - the reality however is that access to information outside of the office allows for 'efficiency' and the ability to check in on your business at all hours of the day. In my case, this early connection to technology led to the habit of tackling opportunities and challenges as they arose, something that has always been called out as a key strength of mine. The challenge in this approach is that it becomes akin to putting on the breathing mask and jumping into the proverbial burning building to fix whatever problem is in front of you at any given time.

Based on my experience in both the corporate and consulting world, the ability to listen intently and to understand is a key trait to embrace for the successful leader. In my case, I was lucky early on in my career to have a mentor that set me straight when required. I recall one of my first performance reviews where I was given some excellent advice. He counseled me on the notion that success in business is only based 10% on the information and knowledge you have, and 90% on how you deal with it. Pretty simple, yet not easily digestible at first for the aspirational young professional attacking the next challenge and opportunity at every turn. With time and practice, that counsel led me to actively listen to what is actually being said in a conversation, what is expected, and what the preferred course of action should be.

With more practice and experience as a leader in business, I've been fortunate enough to pass on the counsel bestowed onto me at an early point in my career through the numerous teams I've led and associates I have had the privilege of mentoring. Mentoring and the ability to listen openly and completely has also taught me an important lesson on empathy. When engaging with others, it is important to understand that many are going through issues and challenges you simply know nothing about. In my own experience of mentoring and challenging my teams to be at their best, I have learned it is always important to be respectful and cognisant to the needs of others. This mantra can be an excellent compass to guide your behaviour and approach to actively listening.

With respect to listening to understand, there are three key messages I would convey to drive success in your career:

Listen to Understand

When faced with a difficult challenge or project, it is natural for many associates to want to take immediate action. Before you 'jump in the fire' and react, ask yourself: do you have all the info you need to solve the problem at hand? Are you addressing what's being asked of you or are you simply doing what you feel is best? Your coach, executives and shareholders may have a different vision of success than you do.

Many leaders can connect the dots and drive a positive outcome based on experience, skill and knowledge. That trait can be very beneficial to you early on in your career but may not serve you well as you progress as a leader. As your circle of influence and accountability grows, you will be much more reliant on the associates around you and as such will need to ensure you have the ability to listen attentively to capture the required information to make an informed decision.

Be Kind and Respectful – Always!

Sounds cliché when you read it, but truer words can not be spoken. Most times you really have no idea what others are up against or going through at any given moment. With that in mind, why not make it a habit of trying to project a positive and friendly demeanour? This can manifest itself in many ways such as providing your full attention during coaching or mentoring sessions, asking your associates and teams how they are feeling, or simply smiling at and greeting others as you pass by – especially those around you in your everyday work and social life. For most, it is natural to do this with those we like and care about but can be a chore to do so with others.

It takes practice to build the skill and commitment to drive this behaviour, but will pay dividends for you in the end. At a large global retailer, they have what is called the Ten Foot Rule – if you come across a customer on the shop floor within this range, smile and ask them if they have found what they are looking for. This simple approach goes a long way to driving a productive conversation and capability of understanding for associates and customers alike.

Know When to Put Your Phone Away

When the expectation is for you to be present and listening attentively, you should not be checking your phone or email during a one to one conversation, dinner with your family or while engaging others at a social event. The burning problem, sports score or entertainment update will be waiting for you when you have the time to give it your full attention. How many times have you been in a meeting where your counterpart is constantly checking their phone or computer?

We've likely all seen associates checking their work email and shutting out those around them while they 'catch up'. In my twenty plus years of corporate life I've seen pretty much everything – associates checking their stock portfolios, texting their girlfriends / boyfriends and even scouring job portals for their next opportunity at another company. My counsel is don't let this be you. If checking your phone or email is more important than the meeting or conversation you are in you need to excuse yourself and leave. That said, there are circumstances where it is perfectly acceptable to take the call – the recommendation is you are upfront with the party or parties you are meeting with to let them know ahead of time that you are expecting a call and may have to excuse yourself.

Takeaways

As you hone your listening skills, be patient. Like riding a bike (or racing a Bigwheel), actively listening and providing your associates, customers and teams with your full attention will take practice, patience and perseverance. Remember to always ask yourself what is really being said and how you will respond appropriately. Happy listening!

<u>3</u>

"Communicate"

The Hospice Story

Almost a decade ago my father lost his battle with cancer. His last days were spent in a hospice, surrounded by friends, loved ones and the odd pint snuck in by the wonderful and thoughtful volunteers on staff. If he was telling this story, he would argue he won that battle, since he outlasted the grim timeline identified by his specialists and doctors by almost six months. His last few months were no doubt very frustrating for him. Before being moved to the hospice and while at hospital, he suffered several strokes rendering him unable to speak. When he first lost his speech, he would gesture for a pen and paper to communicate. Within a day, we had him set up in the hospital with a small whiteboard so he could 'voice' his opinions and carry on a conversation with those around him.

While it took some getting used to the delay in getting his point across, he was very satisfied in this opportunity to continue to the conversation with those around him. Having limited means to communicate also meant his interactions were very crisp and to the point. He would smile and pen "you cheated" while playing cards or "thanks for coming by" when loved ones and friends came to visit. The last couple of weeks he was with us were likely the most frustrating for him during his ordeal. While he still had his full mental capacity with him till the end, he suffered several more debilitating strokes in his last few weeks that rendered him unable to write anything other than simple lines and circles on the whiteboard. The fascinating and frustrating part of this was while we as his intended audience saw a very binary type text on the board of lines and circles, the conviction and articulation of his gestures indicated he knew exactly what he was trying to say. At first, we would ask for clarification – 'what are you trying to say?' which would be followed with an emphatic tapping on the board and pointing at the lines and circles to emphasize the point he was trying to make. Most of the time, we were able to disseminate what he was trying to communicate through seeking clarification in non-verbal cues and gestures. In his last few days, he had given up on the whiteboard altogether and resorted exclusively to pointing and facial gestures to get his point across. His story and experience is a good reminder of the need to adapt and change your communication style and methods based on the changing needs of your audience.

Just like the ability to listen is critical to your success as a leader, your ability to communicate and drive your message is an equally important asset in your leadership toolkit. From spoken word to email to marketing material and corporate presentations, how you communicate and convey your message is critical to promoting your company and your brand. Think back to a business presentation you've witnessed that compelled you to action – was the messaging crisp and to the point or did you struggle to understand what the intent was? My assertion is that it was likely the former. Similarly, think about email direction you've received on the need to perform a certain task or action. I'm sure you can recall times where you've seen examples at both ends of the spectrum – clear, concise and to the point versus wordy, scattered and unclear. In the case of the former, you probably feel pretty confident in what is expected of you, and are more likely to ask for help or clarification if required. In the case of the latter, a scattered and unclear request typically leads to confusion, poor execution and worse – the redirection of that note right to the trash bin.

With respect to listening to understand, there are some key messages I would convey to drive success in your career:

Keep Your Emails Simple and Concise

There is no question email can be very effective tool to get your point across and use for communication and delegation. A simple rule of thumb that has worked for me is keep it to two to three lines, being concise, crisp and to the point as if you were writing on the 'whiteboard'. What is it you are asking for? What is the desired outcome? When is the response required? All of these questions should be defined and articulated in a clear manner to ensure your intended audience knows exactly what action is expected of them. If you can't create a compelling ask or statement in the first few lines, you will have lost your audience and be lucky to get any response at all.

Use the 5-5-5- Rule for Presentations

It was conveyed to me early on that some of the most powerful presenters use the 5-5-5 rule when presenting. Five slides, five bullets per slide, five words per bullet. This is not always possible however, using this type of guideline forces you to keep your most compelling info and hooks for the audience on the slide(s). The rest of the info can be articulated by spoken word during your presentation and linked back to the main themes on the slide. Some of the best presentations, pitches and asks I have seen in my experience with executive interactions were on three pages or less. For some reason I still see examples of associates putting paragraphs on slides, then what feels like a white paper in the appendix. Like in the email example above, you should be concise and simple in your presentation. Sending a twenty-slide deck to your executives for something that can be explained and covered in two does not project the image you want and may cost you the ask.

Follow Up and Seek Clarification

As a busy professional, you will always be challenged to meet deadlines and to keep current at home and the office. Email platforms today almost always have tools and techniques to flag notes that require your attention. Some even offer the ability to add reminders on due dates and when to follow up – use them. For larger and more sensitive initiatives you are working on, make sure you create an environment where you can seek clarification and alignment on what exactly is expected of you. Communication is a two-way street, and seeking clarification and connection on what success looks like as an outcome is a shared accountability.

Seek Face to Face Alignment

Eye contact and the ability to verbalize commitments and actions are key enablers to shared understanding and trust. Where possible, try to finalize alignment of what is expected of you in person. Email is an effective tool, but does not have the context or tone that a face to face conversation can have.

Use and React to Non-Verbal Communication

People tend to say a lot, even when they are not speaking at all. Try to convey an open and approachable attitude when speaking. Avoid folding your arms, rolling your eyes or looking at the floor when speaking or being spoken to. See if you can pick up on the non-verbal cues your colleagues and co-workers are displaying the next time you are in a meeting or presentation with them.

Takeaways

The ability to communicate is a gift, we should embrace it accordingly. Through seeing my father's ability to communicate deteriorate over time, it is something I do not take for granted any longer. The last communication I had with my dad was a smile, something you can pass on to others with no cost or obligation...

<u>4</u>

"Take Time for Yourself"
The Beer Bottle Story

Since my teen years, I have worked non-stop. Whether it was school, sports, the grocery store, the office, in construction, at a restaurant, my house, my marriage or my kids I have worked what seems like three lifetimes already. It is only upon reflection of the number of roles and capacities I've played in that I can clearly think back to a time when I had time to myself. Doing so takes me back to my pre-teen years where I was too old and too cool to be a paper boy any longer but not legally of age to work in a traditional job in retail or the restaurant business.

During this time, I lived in a new housing development in Oakville, Ontario – a growing town just west of Toronto. To pass the time and to keep myself out of trouble, I would sweep through the houses under construction in the evenings and collect the empty beer bottles the workers left behind – a quiet escape for an hour and nice little niche business for an budding entrepreneur.

In hindsight, I don't know how those houses are still standing based on the amount of bottles I collected in the year or so I profited from their consumption. While I was swift and precise about the collection of the bottles to avoid detection from security and lingering workers, I was always respectful of their property and the surprising number of full bottles they would have stashed away for the next day. Perhaps I was still too young appreciate the taste of a pint, given my experience to that point had only been the nasty odd swig of the Labatt 50 my dad would drink while cutting the grass. In any case, I was always meticulous about taking only the empties and leaving the full ones behind. The implicit trust built with the workers I rarely or never encountered formed a social contract I entered at an early age. They would benefit from the odd (or several) pints during the day and I would sweep through in the evening and collect the empties for my benefit, keeping their hiding places and full pints safe from the outside world. I did learn a few hard lessons in the many hours I walked through those houses; things like never go in the cold cellar in a house with no plumbing – yuck!

My days of collecting bottles ended when I started working at the 'Golden Arches'. I did not realize it at the time, but once I got into the restaurant and the 'real world' my ability to take time for myself diminished considerably. Sports and school and girls and all the other trappings of adolescence quickly consumed me as they do most others. As I became longer in the tooth, I was able to maintain time for myself, though it has not always been predictable or as much as I would like or need.

I would not advocate the beer bottle business for my kids given the change in the world and what I would expect to be much different regulations and expectations from construction employers around the consumption of alcohol on the job site. Reflecting back on those beer-bottle-collecting days with a smile, there are few things I would pass on to my twenty-year-old self about finding time for myself if doing it all again; they follow here.

Find Things You Enjoy and Embrace Them

Most of us ultimately find a hobby to take our minds off the daily grind of life. For me, that hobby has been hockey. While I'm dreadful on a good day, I truly enjoy getting out to play. During a normal season I'm lucky enough to get out three times a week to play, plus extra time when my girls are playing or skating. I also have the luxury of coaching both of them, which provides continued hope that we will have a skilled 'McKay' in the family. As I get slower and more seasoned at the game (that's code for 'getting older') I enjoy the opportunity to coach the younger players and seeing the passion and excitement come out in them. The hobby you embrace need not be a sport. For some its reading, for others gardening or collecting – whatever that passion ends up being for you, find it and don't apologize for making time for it.

Secure Quiet, Alone Time for Yourself

This is one that has taken some time to get going for me. Early on in my career I worked almost non-stop, and once the kids came along it became exceptionally difficult to get alone time with my spouse, never mind myself. Over time I adjusted my schedule and found ways to make it work to the point where it is something I have now embraced and cherish. This does not have to be difficult. For me, I make a mental note of a sacred time and stick to it. Finding this alone time does not have to be that often, but is therapeutic. For me, a pint to honour my dad on his birthday (two if I have one for him) or an hour on the deck the odd night when the girls have all retired for the evening to look at the stars helps recharge my batteries.

Spend Time With Loved Ones & Do What They Like

It may sound like this is counter intuitive to making time for yourself, but I find it quite relaxing to let someone else take control every now and then. It sounds easy, but think about the last time you did that. And sorry, eating dinner together twice a week when you're burning the candle at both ends doesn't count by the way. I've been much more methodical about this in the last few months – a great example is letting my kids decide what we do and when. Letting them tell you when we'll be going to the movies or spending the extra hour shagging fly balls after the two- hour baseball practice is over can be quite liberating – try it.

Takeaways

Nobody can really schedule time for you – you need to take the initiative for yourself. Find your passion (or hockey rink, or animated flick your kids want to watch) and find a way to work it into your busy schedule, you'll be well served by it.

For those carpenters, bricklayers and plumbers who instilled the entrepreneur in me I say thank you for teaching me the value of trust and an empty beer bottle at an early and impressionable age. Stay thirsty my friends…

<u>5</u>

"Be Happy vs. Right"
The Results Story

As I mentioned a few posts ago, I left University in my early 20's with a newly minted Bachelor's degree and a take-on-the-world mentality. While I had not yet seen much of the business world, I felt very confident in my ability to solve just about any issue that presented itself. For the first five years of my career I learned a great deal about teamwork, performance, coaching and execution. About five years into my career I was asked to take on a leadership role running continuous improvement for the Canadian division of a large industrial gas company. At the time, we were embarking on a journey that many other large corporations were undertaking – Six Sigma. That period had a remarkable effect on me. While I had always been pragmatic and what I would call process minded, the introduction of a toolbox filled with structure and rigor changed me profoundly. Through the training and certification process, I made it a point to immerse myself in the tools and methodology, becoming a certified Six Sigma Blackbelt myself in the process.

The unintended consequence of this training was a much more linear view of the world around me. I did not foresee this going in, but in hindsight can certainly see how it has affected my thinking and approach to work and life. I began to see many of the business processes and challenges around me as projects and programs with a logical set of steps and methods to work through in reaching an outcome worthy of my own lofty expectations. I began trying to find ways to connect the dots on virtually every program and initiative I was involved in, driving with purpose to improve the condition of my organization and the teams around me. This journey was not without challenge – the downside of having a robust, data driven methodology and set of tools is the continuous strive for perfection. At the time, I found myself trying to squeeze every incremental benefit I could from a process and in turn push my team harder for results on their projects and programs.

Perhaps it was ambition and my stubborn Irish heritage that drove this mindset, aided by the introduction of a new set of tools to validate and shape my position on change management. In either case, I became a product of my environment, chasing perfection and dollars like never before. It was during this time in my career that one of our executives gave me some words of advice I will never forget. During a regular update on the program, he asked me how things were going. We were beating plan, and the project hopper was brimming with potential, yet I found myself concerned and frustrated we were leaving money on the table in existing initiatives we were in the process of closing. As I sought his counsel on what to do about it, he provided feedback I wasn't expecting – he said "there are times it's better to be happy than right" and smiled. I'm sure my eyes glazed over when he said it, yet there was an air of simplicity in this rationale he was providing. While it was a tough journey to transition, I learned to embrace that mantra and know when to leave well enough alone. Taking this road does not imply mediocrity, it merely provides you with the freedom and capacity to direct your attention and talents to where you can do the most productive, meaningful work for your organization.

This mindset is fully transferable to your personal life. Think about a time when you and your spouse, kids, siblings, or friends did not see eye to eye on a particular issue. During a disagreement with a family member, I would encourage you to drift back to that conversation in the office and asking yourself if this is a time you "want to be happy or right'. In my experience, choosing to be happy provides a much better outcome for all involved – a true win-win.

With the luxury of experience comes the opportunity to reflect. As I contemplate how I would convey the lessons learned to my 20-year-old self if I was to do it all over again, there are some key points I would make sure I took notice of.

Know When to Be Happy With Your Result

As stated above, you need to pick your battles. Often times you can drive the results and outcomes you want by tackling the largest chunks of the problem and moving on to the next one. There is academic and empirical research that proves getting your process from 95% to 100% may not be worth the effort. That said, there are exceptions to this rule – you would not want your airline pilot or doctor to be 95% effective. Take a look at some of the Six Sigma readings available readily on line to see more practical examples of this in action.

Know When to be Right

There are some things that are not negotiable. As a leader with experience in multiple disciplines I can say there are some things you simply can not budge on – ethics, safety, the law etc. You will come across events and associates who will attempt to cross the Rubicon on these, be it intended or otherwise. Trust your gut, and act with integrity – always.

Know Your Triggers and Adapt

I've been in many meetings and rooms where someone blurts something out that many in the room know is categorically false. While it can be exceptionally difficult to take the high road and save the conversation and feedback for a later time, you must abstain from calling them out publicly, unless there is immediate danger to an associate's safety or the company's reputation. Your ego will recover if you hold off on providing the feedback, your reputation may not if you decide to call them on it.

Takeaways

This topic can be a difficult one for some. Depending on your profession, education and training you may have considerable challenge in showing restraint or resolve. You may also have to work to control your body language in addition to your verbal cues. Remember, only you can decide when it is best to "be happy vs. right". As you master the skill, you may even find yourself being happy and right....

6

"Build Your Brand"

The Paper Route Story

Around age 10 I took on my first real paying job – as a paperboy. At the time, and like we did a few times when I was a kid (see Chapter 3 - Take Time for Yourself), we moved into a new neighbourhood. At the onset of taking on the role, I had one customer to deliver to one time per week (Saturday). As the neighbourhood was constructed and more owners moved in, the paper route eventually grew to over a hundred papers during the week and just shy of two hundred on the weekend.

Delivering papers was hard work for a lanky kid, but I loved it. Meeting people and delivering their daily dose of the news was a great experience for me. Note for the millennials reading this – there was a time when people actually had to wait to get their news delivered to them – usually a day late, on afternoons during the week and in the morning on weekends – man I feel old! I embraced my role as a young entrepreneur, selling subscriptions in not only my neighborhood, but also in the district my route was in. As a result, I was lucky enough to be selected carrier of the year for my district – a big deal at the time as you got your picture in the paper, a jacket and most importantly an invite to the corporate awards dinner to meet the company brass.

About half of the customers on my route paid their subscription directly to the paper, the other half required manual intervention on my part - a visit every couple of weeks to collect fees for the paper. Through this process I met a lot of interesting people and learned the value of a smile and saying 'thank you'. I learned quickly that a courteous and timely paperboy earned much better tips than one who did not deliver on time or say thanks when paid. I especially liked Christmas time, as customers would provide chocolate, candy and in most cases extra money to say thanks. Good times indeed!

There was a house on my route that was by far my favorite – I can still remember the address today. There was a fancy sports car in the driveway, well manicured yard and fancy modern (for the 80's) interior. The owner was a man I only saw when I collected his payment every couple of weeks. He would always come to the door in sunglasses, a button down shirt and pull crisp bills from his wallet to pay me. I thought this guy was the epitome of cool – his brand oozed of confidence and success. I can tell you his paper was NEVER late or damage – ever. You would take care of that customer too if he consistently paid you double what he owed you.

Fast forward about seven years and I was working in the local grocery store close to that same paper route I cut my teeth on years before. I worked in the produce department, continuing to sharpen my sales skills, only now I was pitching fruits and vegetables I hardy knew about versus the newspaper. From time to time we would have the police visit the store to tend to shoplifters, internal theft and in rare instances actual or attempted robberies. When the police were called to deal with theft or shoplifters, we would often be called up to the cash office to tend watch over the culprit until the police arrived.

On one particular day I was called up the office with a colleague of mine to tend to a shoplifter until the police arrived. When I walked into the office I could not believe my eyes – sitting in the chair in front of me disheveled, embarrassed and crying was the same guy I idolized years earlier as my favorite customer. What's worse, as I looked into his eyes I could see his heart sink, as I'm sure he recognized me from many years before. I remember sitting outside on break after the police came, staring at the guy in the back of the cruiser and trying to piece together what could have possibly happened to him.

What a tremendous fall from grace for the 'coolest guy on my paper route' – a brand he earned over the course of years, with me painstakingly walking up to his front step hundreds of times to deliver his paper on time and undamaged to get my healthy tip in return. In an instant that brand was destroyed, now he was just another shoplifter, being shamed in front of the grocery store in his own neighbourhood, his house only a stone's throw away. The lesson in this is pretty straightforward – it can take years to build your brand, only to have it destroyed in an instant.

The drastic turn of events witnessed that day has stuck with me over the years. Building on that experience and the two decades of corporate life that have followed, I would venture to provide the following suggestions for those seeking to take control of their brand.

Build Your Brand

Every interaction you have is a chance to build your brand into what you want it to be – your coach, co-workers, team members, colleagues, friends, family and loved ones all help frame who you are perceived to be. This is a key point as your brand is actually how others perceive you, not how you see yourself. Some have found this out the hard way. Over the years, I have had associates and colleagues at the office stomping mad about a performance review or 360 assessment they disagreed with. My counsel is always the same – if it was one person penning it and they don't have the guts to approach you, let it go. If you have multiple data points reiterating the same trend or behaviour, you have an adjustment to make. You may not like it, but perception _is_ reality.

Nurture Your Brand

The same interactions mentioned above can be dangerous if you change the perception of others on who you are. Always be mindful of how you are perceived, and never let issues of trust or integrity linger. If you receive feedback you are not happy about, don't try and do a complete 180 on the spot. Take the time to figure out what you need to do differently and adjust accordingly over time. I have seen instances where people take the feedback and completely over index on the opposite behaviour, bringing up even more concern and discussion than if they had of stuck to their old ways. Take a few moments every day to consider how you have helped or hurt your brand today.

Provide Timely Feedback to Others

Awareness is key to building and protecting your brand. If you see instances where someone you know or care about could be putting their brand at risk, take the initiative to let them know in a respectful way. As seen in the example of the customer on the paper route earlier in this chapter, a moment of weakness can have a devastating impact on your brand and future. There is empirical evidence that shows doing something repeatedly forms a habit that is tough if not impossible to overcome. When you see a colleague, family member or associate starting down a path that may lead to a challenge later, you should let them know. You would expect the same in return would you not?

Takeaways

Your brand is like a tree – it is seeded, forms roots and grows over time. Nurture it, prune it where it needs reshaping and protect it. The largest tree in the forest near your house could be over a hundred years old, yet could be gone tomorrow due to a saw, an axe or lightning. Don't let your brand be cut down in front of your own eyes.

7

"Share the Wealth"

The Gum Story

In my late teens, I headed off to London, Ontario to attend University. I learned very quickly what it meant to work to survive. After paying tuition, rent and utilities, it seemed there was little to no extra cash left to go around. While I managed to save some money up and receive government loans to attend school like most others at the time, it was tough sledding.

The first summer I decided working in the grocery store alone was simply not going to provide the income I needed to survive another year at University. Coincidentally, I had a friend who had recently started working in the deck and fence business and needed a partner. The timing was perfect – and the job a much-needed income boost for me. From the first day on the job I was enamoured with the contractor life. I showed up with my new work boots and a hammer on the first day and was immersed into the role.

The company we worked for provided all the tools and equipment we needed; an auger, wheelbarrows, shovels, compressors / nail guns and perhaps most importantly the beat up old pickup we got to drive around for the summer. To this point I had never driven a truck, in this case it was a 1980 GMC Sierra – brown, rusted, heavily used and yet awesome. We named the truck 'Betsy', can't recall why anymore but it stuck. By the third week we had settled in with Betsy, making our regular runs to the lumber yards, customer sites, our shop and the landfill at the end of each job to dispose of the end-cuts and other garbage.

One day we were unloading our garbage at the landfill and a car pulled up in the spot beside us. Since there were three to four parking spots that would be tasked with dumping their trash in the same dumpster, the 'trash' he was removing from his trunk was readily visible to us as we unloaded wood cuts, cement mix bags and other garbage from Betsy. The interesting thing was he was taking the boxes out of his trunk and piling them behind his car, as if to stage them before he threw them in the dumpster. We quickly realized what he was dumping – chewing gum, and lots of it.

When we asked him why he was dumping it he said it was all close to expiry and could not be sold. We asked if we could take it off his hands and he said no – it had to be dumped, based on company policy.

After some pleading and further small talk, he finally gave in. He told us he would leave it stacked where it was (2 feet from the edge of the dumpster), and as far as he was concerned he had done his job. What happened next was pure magic!

Our truck 'Betsy' was only a two-seater – no room for large tools or passengers behind the front seats. We thought for a few moments and proceeded to pull the seats forward and cram every pack of gum from the edge of the dumpster into the truck. From that day forward and for the rest of the summer, we would hand out gum to everyone we met – with the disclaimer that it was saved from the dumpster and would be expiring soon.

Within a few weeks we were treated like rock stars by our suppliers – entering the lumber yard and having the associates line up to load our daily needs. For anyone that has ordered lumber or sorted through it for a project, you know about the inevitable twisted, warped, discoloured and cracked pieces that end up in the top of the pile or on your order. Not so for us - the more the gum flowed the better the service and product quality became.

We handed out gum the entire summer, with some to spare at the end of the season when I headed back to University. Having had another two decades to chew (pun intended) on the experiences that summer, there are a few pivotal pieces of advice I would offer up for your consideration.

Create Your Own Wealth

Not meant in the literal sense here but rather embracing the small wins life offers and making the most of them. We could have simply watched the gum rep throw the boxes in the dumpster – and not had the life experience I'm writing about now, more than twenty years later! Think of your own situation and how you can make the most of what you have. In a world where we are constantly encouraged to crave more and revel in excess, sometimes the next great moment or opportunity is actually right in front of you. Don't let it pass you by.

Share the wealth

Would it have been feasible for us to eat a thousand packs of gum ourselves that summer? Possibly, but that would not have been very practical. By sharing our chewable bounty, we made connections that had a lasting impact for our customers, our suppliers and ourselves alike. Our customers were the beneficiaries of best product from the lumber yard on the day it was picked, and we as impressionable young adults learned about personal connection and building relationships through sharing the gum and the story on how we acquired it. Leveraging that to your situation, think about what you have to offer others and plan to share.

It's the Thought That Counts

Whether its gum, a compliment, a smile or simply saying thank you, sharing the wealth does not have to imply a transfer of money or material items. Rather, you can make someone's day with a simple gesture of kindness and gain personal satisfaction as a result. Think about how you can offer up your time, your knowledge or your shoulder to lean on when someone needs you. Sharing the wealth can be highly satisfying and beneficial for you and those around you.

Takeaways

Every now and then I see an old GMC Sierra on the road and think back to those days. While my trips to the lumber yards and contractor service stores we ruled in our youth are much more infrequent these days, I still smile when I enter the lot. I even see the odd face I recognize from back in the day. At times, I even build up the courage to recommend getting a truck for our next vehicle on the home front. Needless to say, I don't have my truck yet, and don't think I will anytime soon. Until then, I'll just keep chewing gum…

<u>8</u>

"Fight for What You Believe In"

The Fight Story

As a youngster, I was pretty laid back – your average kid with a calm disposition. I was quite content to go with the flow, playing with my friends in the school yard not letting much get to me. I see that same type of laissez faire attitude in my own kids, which reminds me of a much simpler time in life. Growing up I had an older brother, a younger brother and sister living with me. We would wrestle and fight like every other set of siblings I've ever known but those behaviours seemed to only be reserved for our own family.

I remember vividly the first fight I ever got into that was not with my own kin. We had a hill out behind our school which is where all the 'fights' would take place. I was in grade 5 at the time and for reasons that escape me now I ended up on this hill engaged in a pre-arranged tussle with a class-mate. We jostled and exchanged clumsy punches and blows till he fell to the ground, at which point it was over. For those trying to paint a picture in their minds recall we were in grade 5 and uncoordinated at best. This was certainly not mixed martial arts or professional wrestling type theater. Either way the high of that day set something off in me that drove me to be a little more persistent in my approach to life.

Fast forwarding to my career in the corporate world, I can think of multiple examples where this same persistent approach to fighting for what I believe in has paid off. I spent the first fourteen years of my career at the same company, where I had the opportunity to learn new approaches to old problems. As I gained knowledge and experience in how to address them, I found myself much more confident in my ability to stand up for my opinions and back up the recommended course of action with purpose and resolve. While you (hopefully) don't end up coming to blows in the corporate world to get your point across, you do need to be persistent in your ability to fight for what you believe in.

When I returned to the retail business in 2010, I was enamoured with the posters on the walls we would see with quotes from their founder, Sam Walton. One such poster had the tag-line "swim upstream – go the other way". It was refreshing to see this candidly called out since in most businesses, people are reluctant try new things not to mention encouraged to do so. I embraced this mantra whole heartedly. Building on the experience gained in the earlier parts of my career and my growing leadership presence I could drive initiatives that even surprised me. From fuel programs and inventory efficiency to reverse logistics and new ways of bulk merchandising in line I'm proud to have led company and industry changing initiatives. The key success in these programs was overcoming the status quo, or 'we've always done it this way' mentality to drive transformational change.

In driving and implementing these initiatives, my teams and I faced obstacles and detractors which we would overcome. The key to driving these forward and the ultimate success of the programs was continuing to fight for their implementation. Based on my experience in driving change, I would offer up the following recommendations for consideration in driving your own change efforts corporately or personally.

Do Your Homework

Anyone is capable of developing a stance or a position on an issue. The key is to ensure you have the data and information to back it up. A continued knee-jerk reaction or objection to your recommended actions is usually rooted in one of two positions held by the other party: the lazy one ("but we've always done it this way") or the more dangerous passive aggressive one ("that will never work"). Beware of both, for they will slow down progress and if left unabated can kill the initiative. Once you have identified where the resistance is coming from, it is imperative you take the time to listen to their concerns and collaboratively work towards a resolution that you can both live with.

Be Persistent

If you've done your homework and have the information to back up your desired approach, you should have confidence in your ability to fight for what you believe in. This does not necessarily mean inviting your detractors to meet you on the hill after class, but it does entail standing up for what you believe is right for your organization.

Persistence is in my view one of the most underrated attributes of leadership. There are many companies, products and comforts we take for granted that would never have come to be without persistence.

Kids have an uncanny ability to be persistent – I witnessed a very recent example in my four-year-old. Tired of dragging the training wheels around on her bike, she asked me to take them off so she could ride free. I obliged, and she proceeded to hop on her bike and start riding. She needed help to keep her balance, but quickly shooed me away saying I was just slowing her down. She would fall down and get right back up, carrying on down the sidewalk on our street. In less than an hour she was riding on her own and has ever since. We can all think of examples in our own lives where we had the persistence and perseverance to drive forward. Take the training wheels off and make it happen!

Read Your Audience

There are times when your idea or proposal may be ahead of its time or not a desired option for the masses. If any or all of the organization, your peers or your management are not prepared to go with you on the journey, you need to decide if your idea is worth the continued fight. In most cases the answer will be self-evident but in others, you may have to back away, even if you have the data to back up your position and the best interest of your organization in mind. In these situations, it is best to "be happy vs. right".

Takeaways

Since the fifth grade, I've had the opportunity to engage in a few more fisticuffs, but nothing worthy of its own entry in this series. The 'fights' I've had in my career have been much more rewarding than any knockout in the schoolyard could have ever been. Don't ever be afraid to stand your ground and fight for what you believe in...

<u>9</u>

"Be a Champion"
The Pittsburgh Story

Sports has always been an important part of my life, and winning has always been a passion. From a young age I was fortunate enough to play in many different leagues in multiple sports from soccer, baseball, football and finally hockey. While time is catching up with me and my speed and skills are diminishing, I still enjoy getting out and playing various sports.

My first sporting experience was playing soccer. As the son of immigrants from Northern Ireland it was fitting that my parents try to test my skill at 'footy' as my first entry into the sporting arena. In my first year, we absolutely dominated every team we played, enjoying an undefeated season. While the team may have destroyed all takers, I certainly did not have much if any of a part to play in that. As a newcomer to the sport, the coaches put me in at half-back. Not precise or skilled enough to be a striker up front, yet not reliable or quick enough to be a defender. The half-back position suited me well - I learned the game and played well enough not to be a liability to the team.

The next year I told my dad I wanted to try something else, since I had already reached the pinnacle of the soccer world. At that age I did not understand the concepts of persistence, commitment or continued performance growth. In my mind I had already been there done that and did not need to play that sport anymore. Nothing like peaking in your sporting career your first year playing!

Next on the list was baseball. I played three years in a mixed league and don't think I hit the ball once. In my first year, we were dreadful – not winning a game the entire season. Quite the role reversal from the soccer triumph the year earlier. I remember my coach telling us to wait out the pitcher and 'go for the walk'. While I peaked early in soccer, I did not get the chance in organized baseball.

In high school I started playing football. I enjoyed the physical sports quite a lot, and our teams had very good success through my tenure there. The peak for me was winning the regional championship in football my last year of junior and making the final game three of the five years I played. This was a defining moment for me in my early development as a leader, as I learned you could not always do everything yourself – the game and the end prize is much larger than any one player. Every play, tackle and exchange of the ball provided a new opportunity for success or failure, which I embraced.

After I left high school I took up hockey. Strange that as a kid in Canada I skated a ton and played road hockey even more, but never did them both together during childhood. For the first few years I was terrible – let's peg that at one step below dreadful. It seemed like I could skate or carry the puck and shoot but not do both together with any form of success. Being stubborn and persistent I kept with it, to the point that I'm now on the ice three to five times per week depending on the season and my kids' schedule. The peak of my hockey career came this past April – at a tournament away from home no less.

Our first foray into this tournament the year prior saw us lose every game - badly. While many would blame it on the late-night card games, lack of sleep and exploring the city at all hours of the day and night I look back and chalk it up to desire. We were there for a good time, not a long time as the song goes and hockey was secondary for us. Not that there was anything wrong with that.

The second year we went to this tourney we were a different team. Having seen the sights and the local atmosphere the first time around we seemed to be much more focused on hockey. In my case, I was just happy to be skating since I had been off my skates for six weeks prior with an injury. Each game brought us a chance at redemption from the prior year's result, and in the end we went undefeated and won 'the cup'. This win felt good for me – it had been over twenty years in the making!

Looking back on my not so illustrious sports career, there are some lessons that were 100% transferable to my work career. The key points I would pass on follow.

Winning Is Not Easy

I was lucky in my brief but successful soccer career. The same cannot be said for business and personal success in life – you have to work at it every day. While luck can and does play a factor for some, holding out for some good luck in your career and personal life is not a viable approach. In some cases you may have a series of setbacks, a losing streak if you will, but you need to dig deep to find the perseverance to continue. You can be a champion if you play the 'full season' in your work. Like most things in life, you have to put in the work if you want the reward.

Working Hard Does Not Guarantee Success

Early in my career I was of the mindset that hard work would translate into tangible results both personally and professionally. This concept was reinforced with messaging in the media and from childhood mentors and coaches – "work hard and good things will happen." While this holds true for the most part, I can tell you from experience the teams and players get much tougher as you work your way from the minors into the more 'professional' arenas. While the professional wins taste much sweeter the higher you climb in the corporate world, the losses and setbacks can have a lingering effect. The key is to minimize them and work with your team to ensure you win more than you lose.

Play the Team Sports

Winning as an individual is exciting and highly gratifying. On the other hand, winning as a team creates a much longer lasting halo effect and creates the possibility for an amplification effect if you are able to continue to 'play' together. As stated above, the stakes get much higher as you move to the big leagues in the corporate world so having a set of teammates you trust and that can deliver is paramount to your collective success. Like some professional athletes, careers and tenure in a company (or on a team) can be quite long, so it is imperative that you are consistently working to drive the team mandate forward. Having seen this play out over the years, my finding is failure to play your role on the team can leave you looking on from the bench while others thrive. Your job as a leader is to continually draft and empower the team, in the same way a professional sports coach or general manager does.

Takeaways

I am thankful for the opportunities I've had to play sports. More so, I am happy that I have had the chance to experience success and defeat in multiple arenas. The high of winning 'the cup' twenty years after my hockey career started was worth the wait, and highly satisfying. In addition, I think our championship aura and spirit rubbed off on the Pittsburgh Penguins (the local NHL team), as they won the Stanley Cup a couple of months later. Coincidence? I think not – being a champion is contagious...

<u>10</u>

"Take Your Time"
The Peanut Butter Cup Story

Those who know me well can tell you I am a huge Star Wars fan. From an early age I was enamoured with the movies and now later in life have the opportunity to pass on that appreciation and tradition to my own children. The fact that new installments in the series are still coming out is a testament to the longevity of the brand and the storyline.

I was still pretty young when Return of the Jedi came out but at this point I was all in – had already watched the other two movies in the trilogy and when the chance came to catch it in the theater I was excited about the opportunity. My dad took my brother, my sister and I to see the movie early on in its release. There was lots of buzz about the movie (would Luke turn to the dark side?) and certainly lots of anticipation from us on the opportunity to share stories with our friends and act out the scenes during playtime.

This particular night in the movies my dad brought peanut butter cups for us to snack on – a personal weakness of mine that still endures today. The movie theater was dark, the movie was awesome and I was hungry – if my dad passed me a cup I was going to hammer it down the hatch. I started chewing and came to the horrifying realization that something was terribly wrong – I had forgotten to take the wrapper off! I now faced one of the more difficult decisions in my young life – should I spit it out or try to salvage the situation and work around the wrapper to get the peanut buttery goodness separated from it? In the end, I spat it out and was very disappointed in myself. In my haste to eat the treat, I missed a key step in its preparation – the removal of the wrapper. In those days you were lucky to get even one, and since there were three kids and three cups in the pack there was no second chance to get it right. I enjoyed the movie, but still harboured some discontent over the wasted treat.

In the corporate world, haste can yield the same type of disappointment. If you don't take the time to think through your decisions and actions before you implement them, you can find yourself in a jam. In my own experience, I've been told by many coaches, colleagues and team members that I have the unique ability to connect the dots on an issue or initiative very effectively, and within a very short timeframe can develop a plan of action to correct or implement it. While this skillset has served me very well over the years, it can have the unintended consequence of leaving those who may not fully understand the challenge or resolution wondering what exactly is going on.

Over the years I've embraced the need to take the time to listen to the feedback and concerns of others before implementation. While foreign at first to the 'doer' who simply jumps into action, I have found this has been a very rewarding compromise, since the builds and suggestions from others gained along the journey can actually provide a much more meaningful and lasting result than simply plowing through the implementation initially thought out. My transition to the consulting world has only solidified this approach, as it is imperative to listen to customer needs and drivers to appropriately deliver the solutions and value added services they are engaging you for.

While the concept of slowing down and taking your time can be counter-intuitive for the workaholic, I have found there is comfort and heightened performance that comes from practicing a few key habits to drive success. A view on each follows.

Slow Down to Go Faster

If you take the time to bring others along on the change management journey with you, the momentum created with the group can create a tidal wave of support and success during implementation. Schedule time during the implementation to answer questions, address concerns and build alignment. You'll be glad you did, since it provides the opportunity for any early risks or conflicts to get called out before you jump into the effort. Remove the wrapper before you take a bite out of the initiative.

Maintain forward momentum

Slowing down does not imply stopping. I have heard many executives cringe when someone mentions 'slow down to go fast'.

While you may feel the need to slow the machine down to bring others along with you on the journey, you must continue to hit your milestones and drive results. Find the quick wins you can implement to gain alignment and demonstrate success for whatever program you are implementing. It is possible to address concerns and drive the program forward simultaneously.

Seek Feedback

Find trusted advisors to provide timely and effective feedback on your pace and methods. Most detractors to the change or the process won't openly challenge – the more common outcome is withdrawal. Find a way to get the information you need on who to engage and how to help them feel more comfortable – an engaged detractor can become the biggest cheerleader for your initiative if you help make it their idea.

Takeaways

With over two decades of driving initiatives, programs and projects from a focused process level change to corporate wide transformations, I can now appreciate the need to manage the pace at which initiatives move forward. Teams you lead will likely have differing levels of skill, tenure, knowledge and ability to execute. The key for you as a leader is to keep the initiatives rolling and the team motivated.

Nowadays, I find myself very meticulously removing the wrapper from each peanut butter cup I consume. I think I tell my kids the story of the movie theater wrapper every time we eat them; to which they now roll their eyes. In time, I'm sure they will understand the need to take their time…

<u>11</u>

"Have Fun"

The Shopping Cart Story

The time worked in the grocery store during my formative years has provided me with multiple learning moments and reflections on leadership. For the most part, there was a core group of associates we worked with in produce, with little turnover in the staff for the duration of my employment there, almost twelve years in total. In hindsight, and as I've since experienced in my tenures in other organizations, it is very rare to see that low of a turnover. Some of the associates I worked with back then are still employed by the same organization, albeit in different roles or at different stores.

When I think back to that time, I think the secret sauce of our successful retention was having fun. Over time, we found multiple ways to make the most out of our time together at work. One such mechanism we would employ was to seek opportunities to initiate new associates in their first few weeks on the job. A particularly popular initiation involved sending a new associate who had the misfortune of coming over to produce to other departments to find fictitious items like the 'counter stretcher' or 'water washer'. We had an alarmingly high hit rate with these requests, with almost every associate eagerly heading out on their way to find them. Over time, we got craftier in our requests, sending them to one department at a time, saying things like "if the meat guys won't give you one talk to the folks in bakery." We would even go so far as to insist they not come back until they got it.

While the 'counter stretcher' and 'water washer' were local favorites that endured the test of time, my personal favorite was getting new associates to count the wheels on the buggies. Like the others, this one had a very high success rate. To the credit of most of the associates, they would start out questioning the task, but over time we got craftier and more learned ourselves, telling them there was a sense of urgency due to the wheels having to be replaced when the technician came the next day, hence we needed to let them know how many wheels there were. For those that rightly pointed out the ludicrous amount of time it would take to perform the task, we smartly pointed out that they could save time by simply counting the buggies and multiplying by four. Since they would have to go and collect the buggies anyway, they could simply count them and do both tasks at once.

Whatever the initiation task was, there was always a strong sense of bonding created with the new associate. While some initiations at Universities and Colleges have taken a sinister turn, with many ending up with negative press in the media, we were always respectful of the associates involved. That respect and team building contributed to the low turnover and sense of belonging we built for the team.

While I was a teenager when most of these examples got their start, I have continued to see the payback and benefits of having fun in the workplace. Options to bond as a team are endless; it is up to you as a leader to find ways to make it work. Some of my recommendations follow.

Simple Ways to Have Fun Can Have a Big Payback

I've seen birthdays, babies and more celebrated with massive returns on engagement and team dynamics. You don't have to count wheels on buggies or send someone to find the counter stretcher to have fun. In my experience, simply finding ways to get the team together in a non-meeting type environment can have massive benefit. With the changing multicultural landscape we are lucky enough to find ourselves living in, there is always an event upcoming you can celebrate. For me, I have found the opportunity to celebrate some of these events as a team creates not only an opportunity to learn about other cultures (and food!), but also an incredible opportunity to bring the team closer together. This works especially well when you are working in a highly stressful part of an organization or have a particularly challenging program or project you are working on. A little team time can go a long way in helping drive engagement and performance.

Get Out of the Office

While many large companies are cutting back on their outings for employees due to cost and liability constraints, there is still merit in doing an event externally. I've seen bowling, laser tag, barbecues and others used successfully in my career. I would caution that not everyone shares the view of engagement being driven by events held outside the office. I once had an HR manager tell me 'you can't barbecue engagement' during a seminar - to which I put my hand up and passionately disagreed (swimming upstream). In my experience getting out of the office as a team during working hours has a very high impact on engagement and team dynamics. If you think about it, you spend more quality time with the associates at your workplace than you do with your own family – you must find ways to make that time spent productive, fun and empowering so you are not defeated and bitter when you get back to your own family.

Use Sports as a Lever

In my early career, I played in golf leagues, hockey tournaments and softball teams made up of associates from the office. While we often had to fund these ourselves, they provided an excellent opportunity to meet co-workers from different departments, geographies and in some cases even clients. Many companies still operate employee driven social clubs and offer incentives to employees to remain physically active. A corporate gym membership or reduced rate can provide you with the benefit of not only improving your health but also interacting with associates at the office you may not work with on a day to day basis. I still play in tournaments and on teams with associates from my former employers.

Takeaways

Having fun is a universal skill, one that transcends from the grocery store to the shop floor to the board room. While you need to be respectful of others and diligent in the time spent working on a particular task, the payback of having an engaged and cohesive workforce is a very powerful thing. If you're feeling brave you could also ask the produce associate where you can find a 'counter stretcher' on your next visit...

<u>12</u>

"Learn to Let Go"

The Blanket Story

As a kid with three siblings, I had to share pretty much everything from meals to toys to clothes. Those of you with siblings can relate to the challenges of pooled possessions. One thing I did have which was my own was a security blanket. While nobody ever called me 'Linus' as a kid I always think back and envision what I must have looked like dragging that thing around. It was a staple for me in everyday life, providing comfort and a warm snuggle when I needed it. The blanket was orange and white, with 'Raggedy Ann and Andy' on it, I can still picture it now.

By the age of about nine, my parents had concluded that my blanket was a problem for me, and that I was just a little too attached to it. I don't recall taking it everywhere with me, but my siblings tell me I would take it everywhere, to the point where it was getting in the way. In my mind it was more of a bedtime ritual like a stuffed animal.

In any case the decision had been made that I would be parting ways with it. At first my parents tried explaining to me that big kids didn't have blankets and I should get rid of it. That did not work out well for them, my extreme clutching abilities prevented that from ever happening. Over time and as my attachment to the blanket became more of a problem for my parents, they realized they needed to come up with a much more concrete solution – to rip the band aid off so to speak.

The fateful parting of ways came during our annual trek to Myrtle Beach, South Carolina. As we departed the hotel and settled into the car for the long drive home, I could not find my prized sleeping companion. When I prompted the others in the car for its whereabouts my parents simply stated it must have been packed away and we would not be stopping to get it out. Tears and sulking ensued, but the truth was much more painful. When we arrived home, there was no blanket to be found – it was not until some time later that my older brother fessed up to the family's evil plan to leave it behind at the hotel. While I was crushed, I had already moved on and let it go – my parents had succeeded in their efforts to wean me off the blanket.

Fast forward to the current day and the same logic applies. Some of this was articulated in the chapter on "Be Happy vs. Right" so I won't duplicate the message here. What I will focus on is the personal side of things. You will encounter many associates in your career who don't share your point of view, beliefs or vision for the future. Some are your peers, some your staff and others your superiors. If and when you have negative interactions with these folks it is imperative that you let it go and move on. Stubbornly holding onto your beliefs and positions like a security blanket will not help you move the initiative forward if you don't learn to let go and see the other side of the discussion.

Having seen multiple examples of situations involving and around me of not letting go at the opportune time, there are some key pieces of advice I would convey.

Champion Your Cause, Then Move On

The business world moves very fast – you must make your pitch, implement your desired changes and move on. Resting on the laurels of your last success or waiting patiently to have your pitch embraced is short-lived and short-sighted. I have seen this amplified in the consulting field. As I look to leverage my experience in the corporate world for the masses I have found times when a proposal to transform a client's current situation lingers. There are potential clients that I meet who are in desperate need of transformation, yet preoccupied with other priorities. When talking about it with a mentor recently, she reminded me of my own priorities a short time earlier as a supply chain executive. While there are many items on the to-do list, the one you are pushing may not be at the top of the list. Make your case and move on.

Things Will Not Always Go Your Way

Despite your best efforts, you may not be able to convince others to move forward with your initiative or proposal. If you have outlined your position to the best of your ability and still don't find a champion or team members to move forward with, you need to move on. Let it go, minus the sulking and tears of course. There are times when those projects and proposals are resurrected. When and if that happens, the same principles apply. Update your pitch, champion the cause and then move on.

Pick Your Battles

I've seen the unfortunate example of an associate not supporting a new initiative put forth because the team in question did not support theirs. While this may seem like a legitimate approach – I don't see how it can ever end well for the proponent. As a leader, it is your job to do what is best for the team and the organization. While you may not always get your way, you need to take the high road and set the example for your team. I've seen this play out at all levels of organizations. The petty grudge and sour taste does not end at the water cooler unfortunately. The higher the grudge goes in the organization, the more dangerous the outcome in my experience.

Takeaways

While we are all a little older now, I still make the trek to South Carolina with my family just about every year. About a decade ago we started staying at a newer hotel in the north end of town. As fate would have it, the same old hotel my blanket was left in sits right beside it. While the old hotel may be dwarfed by the new high rise condominium that's been constructed adjacent to it, there's still a part of me that wants to go back to the front desk and ask to check the lost and found. On second thought, its probably time to let go...

<u>13</u>

"Be Present"
The Iconic Leader Story

This chapter contains some of the most poignant advice I've given to those I've mentored over the years. Having had the privilege of working in large companies and experiencing aspects of various roles from the shop floor to the board room I have had the luxury of seeing many different characteristics, personality traits and approaches to getting noticed.

We are all familiar with the larger than life personality in the organization that commands a level of respect and aura every time they walk in the room. Whether it is the rank of the associate within the organization or the track record they bring, there are certain individuals that just have the ability to take control of the situation and instantly inform all of their presence.

In my early years in retail, this would manifest itself in the executive walk through visits at the store. When these visits occurred, I could never understand all the fuss for the brass coming through. Why wouldn't we just have it look good all the time? With more experience in business, it became clearer that the level of performance expected during those visits was very hard to sustain while meeting corporately imposed budgets and financial targets. In the office setting, the concept of being present came out in what seemed like endless drafts and rehearsals of presentation materials for the C-Suite of the companies in question. Teams had to know who to play what verse to in the presentation and anticipate the reaction and questions that would certainly follow. All it would take is one shot across the bow from the key stakeholder in the room to kill or derail your entire idea – sound familiar?

The other interesting phenomenon I've seen in the last decade is the concept of there always being another layer to the onion or put simply the bigger fish analogy. Even if you are persuasive enough to get your proposal, program or concept over the line, I've become increasingly aware of the impact the parent organization can have over the regional or geographical play. Having seen this play out in boardrooms at multiple companies the bigger fish analogy transcends both industry and C-Suite tenure. Add to that the added layer of shareholders, activist investors and fierce competition and the bigger fish analogy truly comes to light.

My experiences have had a truly profound impact on my understanding of the business world and my approach to being present. When I give counsel to my mentees about how to approach the desire to be noticed in the organization, I talk to them about the levels of presence I've come to understand, the need to seek those who have a presence in the organization and the requirement to master the art through repeated practice.

The Three Levels of 'Being Present'

When seeking to get noticed in an organization, there are three levels of 'being present' that I like to refer to; the first is about being seen and heard, the second being asked your opinion and the third and most valuable is about being sought out before the program or initiative can continue. What follows is some commentary and reflection on each. I like to think of them as a hierarchy, and in my experience have seen associates move through them as they mature in their confidence and abilities.

Being Seen and Heard

We can all think of the associate or co-worker who must always get a word in edge wise. Whether the commentary they are adding provides value or not, they just can't stop themselves from speaking up. These associates may choose to talk more or less depending on who is in the room with them to ensure they are noticed. This type of presence is direct and hard to miss, since they play a very active part in the interaction or meeting. The danger of not moving out of this stage of the hierarchy is you may find yourself left out of important sessions if the commentary you provide does not add value. How many times have you sat in a meeting and rolled your eyes or prompted a co-worker when this individual gets going?

Being Asked Your Opinion

The second level in the hierarchy of being present is having your opinion sought out. Usually it involves someone calling on you for advice – "nobody knows this better than you, what do you think?" Think of this in a C-Suite or key customer setting. Are you being allowed to simply read your scripted slides or are you being asked to provide your candid advice. I've seen this manifest in been asked "if it was your money would you spend it?" The key differentiator in this stage of the hierarchy from the first one is you don't have to be vocal in the room to be noticed. By this point, your reputation and subject matter expertise speaks for itself.

Being Sought Out Before Moving any Further

The highest level in the hierarchy is being the sought-after approver or expert to move forward. This comes naturally with rank for most senior executives, but when thinking of it from the management level being personally sought out for your expertise before the program in question can move ahead exudes a high level of presence for you as the expert. The downside of this highest point in the hierarchy is being pulled in multiple directions at once. Most busy associates and executives learn early on you can't be everywhere at once. The key here is to make sure you have the ability to transfer knowledge to your team and your peers so you can be sought for signoff or counsel before the initiative proceeds versus being the go-to for everything.

Seek Those Out Who Have a Presence

There are natural leaders and associates within all companies who exude an aura of presence. Some call it charisma; others would call it being an extrovert or expert. Either way, I would recommend finding a way to engage them and build a rapport to gain insight into what makes them possess the power of presence. I have had mentees and associates tell me they are intimidated by these types of people and seek advice on how to approach them. In my experience the best way is to simply find

common ground and ask them to talk about their expertise –
something these individuals have no problem doing. Try it for yourself,
the approach is actually pretty straight forward – "Hi Joe, I saw you
speaking on presence today at the leadership meeting. You seem to
know a great deal about how to approach it, I was hoping you could
give me some tips so I can learn from an expert such as yourself…"
Flattery and the opportunity for 'Joe' to tell you all about how he got to
be so awesome is usually an excellent icebreaker. Though few admit it,
associates love to talk about their strengths, especially when sought out
by an associate who asks the 'how did you get to be so awesome' as an
intro.

Practice, Practice, Practice

While you may not believe it, you wield much more power in every
interaction than you may think you do. If you have an awareness of the
three levels of presence above, and you have mentors and go-to
associates who can provide candid feedback on your ability to build
and exude presence, you have the leeway to grow your presence with
every interaction. The next time you are in a meeting, take the time to
determine who is functioning at each level of the hierarchy. Also take
the time to establish where are you in the hierarchy – what are you
doing to move yourself up the curve and into the third level?

Takeaways

As I said at the start of this chapter, this is one of the key areas of
focus I have with almost all associates and colleagues that I mentor. It
has been very rewarding to see folks who were shy and in some cases,
complacent come out of their proverbial shells and exude confidence
and presence over time. The ability to move through the hierarchy is
completely within your control. I challenge you to take the time to
become self aware of your place in it and improve your position and
potential outcomes accordingly.

<u>14</u>

"Be Safe"

The Seat Belt Story

During my time in the logistics world in my twenties I had the luxury of meeting many seasoned transport and logistics professionals who were kind enough to share their knowledge and experiences with me. From my coach, peers, staff, drivers and vendors I was able to amass a large repository of industry information over my first few years in the industry.

During my tenure at the industrial gas company, I had the luxury of attending and presenting at many safety meetings and events. For us, safety was not just a poster on the wall or something you 'should think about' but rather a condition of employment and price of entry for our supplier partners. I recall fondly a regional manager and former mentor of mine who would start off meetings by asking "what was the first thing you did when you got in your car or truck this morning?" When the answer "put on my seatbelt" was uttered he would ask why? The answers ranged from "it's the law" to "it's a habit". I must have watched him explain a dozen times that while both are true, the latter is more reflective of the reason why. Yes, there are penalties for not doing it but the fear of having to pay those penalties drives the behaviour of putting on the belt which if done "29 times in a row becomes a habit". He had such a passion for safety that it was contagious to all around, and supportive of the culture we had in the company.

A further example of our safety culture was the insistence on backing into parking spaces. We had courses and reminders constantly on the need to not only drive safely, but park safely as well. If you could not find a way to drive through into a spot, we were always coached to back in. I remember vividly seeing suppliers and visitors asked to go back out to the parking lot to back their vehicle in if they had failed to do so the first time around. The associates in the plant had a fair but firm approach to ensuring that compliance to the safety policy was adhered to before the meeting even began. Some vendors would grumble about it but eventually they would respect the policy. The habit of backing into a parking spot held true not only for company vehicles as a company policy but also as a strong recommendation for us to use in our personal lives.

Since those early days I have always backed into a parking spot. I've now done it so often I don't even think about it any longer – its an automatic behaviour. I truly believe that the need for safety is not negotiable in business. Safety is a core value for most companies, and a top priority for our families and loved ones to ensure they make it home each day. Some of my core values on safety are explored in the following section.

Safety is a Prerequisite to Doing Business

Whether its for a large transportation bid or a new lane you are bidding out, safety should be the first consideration not price. When I led transportation for a global retailer the number one ranking criteria I set for the team for selecting a carrier was safety, not price. Like the vendors back in the day being asked to go back out to the lot and back their cars in before the meeting could begin, I wanted to ensure my existing and potential carrier partners know that an exceptional attitude toward safety and the processes and culture to back it up would be a cost of entry, not a nice to have.

Safety is Foundational to Your Personal Life

Your commitment to safety does not end at the office. From checking your smoke detectors to ensuring you have the appropriate safety gear in your home for an emergency (fire extinguishers, first aid kits etc) you must make safety a priority and a habit. We see constant reminders in the media about the need for this diligence about safety. Whatever you find yourself doing outside of work, be sure to spend the extra time to ensure you and your loved ones make it through the day and home safe.

Back Your Vehicle In When Parking, Always

While this was talked about above, I am reiterating here for effect. I can attest to witnessing two accidents in front of my own properties where the vehicles of family members were involved. In both cases, backing the vehicle into the spot initially would have avoided the accident. You must back the car up to get in or out of a spot most of the time, why not back it in to avoid the accident coming out? With back up cameras and collision avoidance in today's vehicles, there is no longer a reason not to do it. You are simply twenty-nine occurrences away from making it a habit!

Takeaways

Safety is ultimately a way of life and way of working. How you develop habits that make you a safer worker, driver and person are ultimately in your hands. The next time you get in your vehicle and put your seat belt on ask yourself why you did that. You have already chosen to make safety a habit by performing that simple act, now you just need to find ways to make it a broader part of your daily ritual.

<u>15</u>

"Know Your Worth"

The Cottage Story

Throughout most of my adult life my family and I have spent portions of our summer vacation in a sleepy town in Bruce County, Ontario. We enjoy the laid-back way of life, the opportunity to relax for a period of time and of course the sandy beaches and award-winning sunsets.

Over the past ten years, we have owned two different vacation properties in the area. In both cases, we did not live in either house full time and had a property maintenance company come and cut the lawns, perform yard cleanup in the spring and fall, snow plowing in the winter and other odd jobs as they arose. I still remember having the owner of a company out to quote on the lawns when we were getting settled into our first property in town. When I asked him how much it would be to cut the lawns he thought about it for a moment and said "thirty bucks". I didn't know it at the time, but that rate would ultimately be his price for every job he did, no matter the size or complexity. As time went on I would pay him for several weeks in advance since we did not know if we would see him and wanted to provide the courtesy of paying in advance. On the days I was on vacation and home when he arrived, I would be sure to be waiting on the porch when he finished with pints in hand to toast a job well done.

On a number of occasions, I asked him why he charged the same rate for everything he did. His answer was simple – "that's what I always charge". I've thought about it a few times since our last interaction and it still surprises me that he does not know his own worth. Surely a fall cleanup is much more labour intensive and hence a higher value as compared to a standard grass cutting.

The same lessons hold true in the corporate world. When I was recruiting and hiring senior level talent I would get frustrated when we were able to pay an outsider a higher rate than somebody we promoted from within because of the internal rules and guidelines on pay. If someone from the outside could be paid X, wouldn't the internal candidate with the tribal knowledge and experience on the inner workings of the organization be worth at least that amount?

In my own experience negotiating pay, whether for a role in the corporate world or for services provided on the consulting side, I have come across the same questions around how to attribute the 'value' of the services being provided. In the case of an existing role or engagement, the salary or rate of the incumbent or prior associate or firm likely drives a big portion of the decision on rate. For a new engagement or position, the key is to determine the value you will be providing, be it as an employee or contractor. Either way, it is important that you are acutely aware of your value in the market and your alternatives before signing yourself up for something below your worth.

In the case of the contractor cutting my lawn up north, he never changed his rate in the ten years we used his services. While we ended up making sure he got what he needed in the end, I was amazed that he never asked for more. When prompted why he never changed his rates he told me he has a very difficult time doing so and typically loses business when he tries to increase them. Ten years is a long time to go without a raise!

There are ways to determine and protect your worth to the market. Based on my corporate and personal experiences with worth, there area a few key considerations to take into account:

Know Your Worth

With the rapid advances in access to information, establishing your worth is much easier today than it has been in years past. Be sure to use market indicators and contacts to determine what your services are worth. If you're in the corporate world, recruiters and peers in the industry can be excellent resources to determine the going rate for your type of expertise, even if it is only in a range.

Receive Fair Value for Your Services

If you know you are being compensated below your worth, speak up! Provided you have the relevant comparable information from point one above and have the track record to back up you're ask, go for it. Recruiters are great examples of associates who help drive fair value for services. Without fail, one of the first questions they ask is about levels of expected and previous compensation. They are using this not only to determine your suitability as a candidate for the role they are considering, but also to determine fair value for a pool of associates with similar transferrable skills. When seeking a change in compensation or role to reflect your worth, be sure to be respectful and on point, with data and examples to back up your ask.

Find Ways to Increase Your Worth

Whether through corporate education programs or courses and designations you fund yourself, find ways to improve your skill base and increase your worth. Many employers offer educational programs that cover costs of courses or programs through accredited learning facilities. Check with your employer to see what your options are. You won't get any help if you don't ask!

Takeaways

As you think about your 'worth' to your organization or clients, think back to the contractor cutting the lawn. You may be satisfied with the 'that's what I've always charged' approach, but you may find your time and skills are worth a whole lot more than even you imagined…

<u>16</u>

"You Never Know"

The Change Management Story

Early on in my professional career I had to learn and embrace change. While it was difficult to grasp the pace at which things change in my first years there, I quickly became quite adept to expect the unexpected. In hindsight, I attribute the ability to adapt to change seamlessly to the fast paced logistics centre I was working in early on in my career. Each call or contact into the logistics centre became an opportunity to engage clients and drive performance for our company.

One example that comes to mind was a colleague of mine who I worked closely with for many years. He had been with the company over twenty years when I started, and was a fountain of information and knowledge for me and the other associates on the team – I looked up to and relied on him constantly as a key resource. One day, we had an interaction that would impact us both significantly for years to come.

On this day in particular, I was sitting in my office at my desk and he came in to talk as he often would. There was however a different tone to his voice that I did not pick up on at first. He sat down and we talked small talk for a few minutes, the gist of which I do not recall. What I do remember to this day is the change in tone and the comment he made saying "there are some people around here who tend not to do much and yet get a lot of credit for it". At first I could not believe what he was saying or if he was even talking to or about me. Any doubts I had were removed when he stood up and said "I'm watching you…" before he walked out. I was stunned – nobody had ever talked to me that way in an office setting and I had absolutely no idea what he was talking about or where he was coming from.

The reason why this interaction would change our professional careers forever is that unbeknownst to him and by absolute coincidence I had signed a contract earlier that day to move to and lead a different department. Not earth shattering by any means but in this case the very person sitting in my office a few minutes earlier and uttering those words would later that day find out he was now a direct report of mine. I knew from previous interactions with him that he was looking to explore other opportunities in the organization but had no idea he had been harbouring such feelings. Was it really about me or just frustration that he had not found what he was looking for? I pondered it after he left my office – the feedback was a complete shock, but direct and to the point which I have always asked for.

When the announcement was released and word got out about the change he returned to my office. His tone had shifted yet again and this time he asked if we could forget our conversation from earlier in the day. There was a long pause as I contemplated how to respond. For reasons that escape me now, I uttered a line I had never used before, yet have used many times since. I looked him in the eye and told him I had already let it go but did not stop there. I told him that my ways of working were simple – we did not have to be best friends, but did have to deliver on our results. "In fact, I don't care if you sh!t in my desk drawer, as long as we deliver on what we need to get done, you and I are good…and if we can have some fun doing it along the way, all the better".

What happened over the next few years was the start of a very important journey for the two of us. We became close colleagues, and I had the luxury of honing my mentoring skills and building trust with someone who had uttered those strange words in my office only weeks prior. As I got to know him better, I found out that his comments on that day were borne out of frustration in his own career. He ultimately wanted to work in a completely different part of the business and had not had the opportunity to do so in the past. In time, and by working together we not only exceeded on delivering results for our department and the organization, but also managed to get him transferred into his preferred occupation in the company. He actually retired from the organization in that role, after spending almost ten years in it.

While challenging conversations in the workplace are nothing new, the lessons learned in this chapter had a deep and profound impact on my leadership style. Looking back at this experience and having had the opportunity to mentor many associates who were and are striving for their next opportunities, there are a few key learnings that stick out for me:

Think Before You Speak

It would have been easy for me to respond negatively and harshly to the comment that he made in my office that day. I think the fact that I was stunned and couldn't believe he was actually talking that way to me forced me to pause and reflect. Think back to a situation in your own career where you have had a challenging conversation at work – how did you react? If you could have it over again would you respond differently? I'm still thankful that I took the time to reflect and coordinate my response since we are both far better off than what could have happened had I instinctively reciprocated with a negative reaction.

Be Respectful, Always

As pointed out in Chapter Two it is highly likely that most folks you meet are fighting a battle you know nothing about, hence you should be kind and respectful at all times. In this case, doing so resulted in this associate landing the role he had been longing for and me being able to further develop my listening and mentoring skills. Since that interaction I have continued to search for the real meaning of what my mentees are asking for. You always need to dig deeper to find true intent and meaning. As I have continued to hone my leadership skills one of the number one observations I have found is the level of frustration amongst associates at all levels of the organizations I work with. While this may manifest itself in a way that is managed through sports and in some cases therapy or counselling, I think I was very naïve early on. Most times, associates are simply looking for a sympathetic ear and in some cases a mentor or champion who will help take on their cause. Listen closely to what your associates and peers are telling you – you might be surprised.

You Never Know

You should always be mindful of 'seeing around corners' and knowing your audience. Your world can change in an instant – a bad day, a misplaced comment or a new boss can all happen to you in the same day. Be mindful of your surroundings and your actions at all times to ensure you are always seen at your best. As covered in Chapter Six, your brand and reputation can take years to build but a nanosecond to destroy. Always keep your composure and think about your actions – how is your intended message being perceived by those on the receiving end?

Takeaways

This story is one of my favorites which had an outcome I am most proud of as a leader. The opportunity to take a potentially volatile situation and transform it into a multi-year mentoring engagement is very fulfilling. I have also had the luxury of building on the experience and leveraging it over the years. As mentioned earlier in this chapter, I've used the "you can sh!t in my desk drawer" line several times since that day. Some associates on my teams have even gone so far as to leave plastic dung in my desk to test the theory. Less stink, but the same shocking impact…

17

"Stay Calm"

The Pager Story

Throughout my career, I've held some very demanding and taxing leadership roles – from the logistics and transport field where your reputation lives and dies on your last delivery, to the sales world where one poorly executed meeting or ill-timed comment can kill the deal, to continuous improvement where your recommendations require signoff by the most senior change agents in the company. I have often been asked how I can remain calm in the most frustrating and dire of circumstances. The short answer is experience, and lots of it. From running a national logistics service centre in my early days for an industrial gas company to leading the Canadian Transport team for a global retailer, I've been very fortunate to learn the ability to remain calm even when multiple things seem to be going astray all at once.

One example that comes to mind takes me back to my late twenties and the cottage (or 'camp' as some would refer to it) we owned in Bruce County on the shores of Lake Huron. Being on the water was majestic, with the soothing sound of the water lapping up against the shore and some of the best sunsets I have ever witnessed. One of the only downsides of this cottage was that we sourced our running water for the cottage (sinks, toilets, etc.) from the lake via a line run about fifty feet into the lake and drawn up to the cottage via a pump. After any sort of a storm or heavy use of the water the intake line would get gummed up with seaweed and other lake particulate that would gather at the inlet valve. Every week or so I would have to venture out about waist high and clean it off to ensure we had adequate pressure in the cottage.

One day I had what I would call the trifecta of challenges to manage. It was (Canadian) Thanksgiving weekend and we were hosting several folks at our cottage. The water line started losing pressure and I found myself having to make the cold and damp trek about fifty feet into the water - in October Lake Huron can be a very unfriendly place; add to this the fact that it was raining and you had the makings of a not-so-fun venture out into the lake. As I stood waist deep in the frigid October waters labouring at the intake valve I heard someone calling my name from up on shore. It was dusk so it was hard to make out the voice with the impending darkness and the sound of the water crashing on the rocks in front of me.

As the voice became more audible I could recognize my mother-in-law coming down the embankment of the yard towards the water. She was holding my pager (don't see many of those around any more do you?) and calling my name. "Your pager is going off" she said. Nice – not only was I stuck in the frigid water cleaning the intake on the line fifty feet from shore, but now I had the office calling to address an emergency. In those days the on-call resource for our emergency response line (accidents, incidents and product releases) had to carry the pager and respond twenty-four hours a day seven days a week. On this weekend, the accountability was mine and by sheer coincidence it was going off while I was waist deep in the lake.

I scowled at the shoreline as I finished with the intake line and made my way back to land. I answered the page and addressed the emergency. Afterwards my wife chuckled as she reflected on my situation. In hindsight, I think I was happy just getting out of the frigid water and being able to make the call from inside the toasty cottage. In any case, that day taught me a lot about keeping calm under pressure. As my career advanced, I found myself in many more pressure-cooker situations. That day was instrumental in helping me learn to contain my frustration and deal with the situation at hand. The key leadership lessons that emerged for me and that I have used successfully since are the following:

You Will Get Through the Challenge

Life hands you many curve balls and surprises capable of making you lose your composure. If you take the positive approach that you can get through it, and know that there is light at the end of the tunnel (and not a train!) you will be in a much better place to manage through the challenge. While this may seem anecdotal and inappropriate when the actual challenge is in front of you, it is imperative that you see the big picture and have the emotional fortitude to realize that this too will pass.

Pressure Can Bring Out the Best in You

I have found that over the years I tend to excel in a pressure filled environment. While not for everyone, finding a way to expect the challenging situation and grind your way through it can be an incredibly rewarding experience. An acute ability to excel under pressure is also an important leadership trait. As you demonstrate your strength and fortitude in delivering in even the most challenging circumstances, you will provide yourself the opportunity to grow personally and professionally. The simple way to approach this is to ask yourself this question: If you know you will face challenges in your life, why get frustrated when they happen? Embrace them and enjoy the ride!

Keep Your Composure

Losing your cool in a pressure filled situation only lessens your ability to deal with it and lengthens the timeframe in which you will feel frustrated. Take the time you need to calm down and get your headspace set to tackle the problem. I still have moments where I slack at this and show my frustration through negative body language or facial expressions. While it's hard to supress your emotion, it is exponentially harder to bring calm and order back to a situation in which you have lost your cool. Where possible and where required, leave the room or take a quick break to hit the reset button.

Takeaways

For most people, staying calm is easier said than done. Over time and with practical experience, you will find your preferred way to handle stressful situations and keep calm. Think of a situation where you were completely stressed out and wish you could have reacted differently. Would taking a few moments to reflect have helped you? Did the experience help you grow as a leader? Did you embrace the challenge or act defensively? The answers to all of these questions can yield a framework for how you approach a challenging situation the next time around. Stay calm and embrace the challenge!

For more examples of challenging situations I have faced in my own career and how the learnings from those experiences can help you in your career, visit the media page on our website at www.avleca.com and click on the FREE links to the "Be Ready" series, where I write about some of the most challenging situations I have found myself in over the years.

<u>18</u>

"Travel Well"

The China Story

One of the most rewarding experiences of growing a business and gaining professional experience is the ability to see different parts of the world. Whether for business or pleasure, I thoroughly enjoy the opportunity to visit new places and explore new cultures, landmarks and culinary experiences. One of my favorite travel experiences in recent years was travelling to the interior of China. While most business trips to the region by western companies (including two former companies I have worked for) are to the traditional business hotspots of Shenzen, Hong Kong or Beijing, I had the distinct pleasure on one of my more recent trips to visit the City of Nanchang in Jiangxi province. A 'small' city by Chinese standards, we were amazed at the amount of traffic (mostly scooters) and sheer vibrancy of the streets as we walked them daily.

I was fortunate on this trip to have my family with me and had pulled my oldest daughter out of school to join us on what would be an experience of a lifetime. When we expressed our concern to school officials about pulling her out of class for two weeks to go on the trip, their response was quick, direct and impactful: her teacher said "she would learn more in the two weeks in the interior of the Country than she would that entire school year in class". I did not appreciate the significance of those comments at the time but soon would.

Being in Nanchang had a notably different feel than some of the other Chinese cities we have visited in the past. While foreigners are present in most of the large cities due to business and personal travel we were what seemed like the only western travellers in Nanchang at the time of our visit. We would walk down the street and literally stop traffic. People would come up to us and ask to have their picture taken or simply touch us. It was particularly strange for my daughter who had an endless barrage of residents asking to touch her hair and have their picture taken with her.

At first it was very uncomfortable but within a few days we became used to the attention and the constant looks and photo requests. My daughter found it particularly flattering and seemed to bask in the attention she was receiving. As we ventured out a little further from the hotel each day, we found the courage to take in the local markets, restaurants and culture. At first it was very intimidating since we did not speak any Mandarin, nor did we have our guide with us when we chose to venture out alone. Over time, and as our confidence grew we would explore the city streets for hours at a time. It is amazing how humans can ultimately find a way to communicate and purchase goods, services and food with absolutely no understanding of the language.

When I tell the stories to friends and family they have a common ask – what was the secret to our success? In short, and in line with the stereotype, I have to say 100% it was the Canadian brand we walked around with. Whether it was the flag on a backpack, clothing we were wearing or the conversations we would have in broken English and Mandarin, we were embraced with open arms when people found out where we were from. In the same way you have a brand that you convey and build on each day, your country does too. While I'm a proud and patriotic Canadian and have visited multiple countries and continents in my years, I was taken aback in China by the amount of value the Canadian brand carries.

While we saw and experienced multiple things that differed from home, we quickly learned to appreciate that we were merely guests in this majestic place - the Canadian thing to do I suppose. As a result, we indeed had the trip of a lifetime as a family. Most times when travelling for business you simply do not have the luxury to explore and enjoy the local experiences of the place you are visiting. In this case, we had two full weeks to take it all in! Some of my personal favorite experiences were engaging with the local street vendors on their wares, trying new cuisine, exploring the local landmarks and shopping centres, and simply finding a way to engage in friendly conversation with the residents that approached us inquisitively.

As stated earlier in this chapter, this particular visit opened my eyes to not only the value of the Canadian brand abroad, but also the need to understand your place as a guest in a foreign country. Some key points we took away follow.

Travel Well

When you are visiting a city or country away from home remember that you are a guest and not the one making the rules or defining cultural practices. Be respectful of the local customs and requests within reason, even if they make you feel uncomfortable at first. On a domestic flight within China on a national airline the flight attendants asked if they could touch my eldest daughter's blonde hair. Strange yes, but she felt like a star in that moment with the attention she received. After spending a week in Nanchang prior to this flight, we were well versed in the curiosity and interest in our family.

Communicate!

Even if you don't know the language or native tongue in the place you are visiting, find a way to communicate and connect with the people around you. In our case, we found that a simple smile started us off on the right foot with all we met. Most of the time, the people trying to speak to us would point at their phones – we quickly learned this meant they wanted to take a picture. By the end of our first week we were in restaurants off the beaten path ordering and eating with the locals. It helped that most of the menus had pictures you could simply point at. If we had not of had the courage to venture out and ask for recommendations on where to eat we would not have been provided the rich culinary and cultural experiences we still talk about as a family.

Grow Your Perspective

Immerse yourself in the culture and sights when you are visiting a new country. In our case, and when the opportunity presented itself, we would ask the English speaking associates in the hotels about where we should visit to get the most out of our experience. They were always happy to recommend popular venues, sites for shopping and restaurants that did not disappoint. For our part, we were surprised that most of the questions we got asked by those who did manage to speak English were about our Toronto basketball team.

Takeaways

Travelling is a fact of life for most professionals in an increasingly small world. It also remains a valued pursuit for leisure and downtime for most people I know. If you can find a way to embrace every trip as a learning experience you will no doubt enrich your life experience and learn a few things along the way. With some luck and communication, you can reciprocate with those you meet. Travel Well!

<u>19</u>

"Be Respectful"

The Produce Story

One of the first life lessons most kids are taught is about respect. Whether it is toward your parents, siblings, peers, authority, your elders or your sports opponents, it is a widely accepted norm in society to be respectful of others. As this skill grows over time, one tends to have a moral compass develop that acts as a guide to determine how you and others should act. When you are placed in a situation that challenges that respect, your compass tells you that something is not right.

I learned the practical application of respect in my late adolescence. At the time, I was caught up in a multitude of life events that occupied my time; from wrapping up my undergraduate degree at university to building fences and continuing to work in the grocery store. One day, while working in the store I received the proverbial tap on the shoulder advising that I should apply for a particular role at head office in my field of expertise at the time – produce. I was excited about the opportunity to join the corporate world, and as outlined in earlier posts in this series, I was feeling particularly confident in my capabilities at this stage in my life.

In preparation for the interview I did many of the things you see job seekers doing today – I carefully crafted my resume, cleaned up my appearance and rehearsed the delivery and messaging of my accomplishments. When I got to the interview at head office, I was as prepared and confident as I could possibly be. During the interview there were two company representatives in the room, one was the human resources representative and the other was the hiring manager. The role was for a junior management role in pricing, and based at the head office on the west side of Toronto.

I thought the interview was going well - really well in fact. They were asking the questions I thought they would, and I had provided answers that I had rehearsed many times over already. During the final stages of the interview, I was asked if I had any questions. One of the things that had been nagging at me was the thought of moving on from my friends and co-workers at the store to a manager role at head office. On the one hand, I was smart enough to know that I would have to leave the store if I wanted to work full time in head office, but on the other was reluctant about leaving my friends and support system behind. Many of us had been working together for over five years and while that may not seem like a long time, it was over a quarter of my lifetime thus far and almost all of my formative years. At very least I wanted to make sure I had an out to return to the store in the event the corporate role did not meet my expectations.

Rightly or wrongly I asked the question – could I still work at the store if I accepted the job at head office? A legitimate question in my mind and worth a shot, even though I knew it would not be a likely scenario. The hiring manager leaned in, folded his hands together and said "don't worry about them, you are going to be one of us now". I couldn't believe my ears – while his intent could have been to put my mind at ease about making the transition, I construed his comments to be openly disrespectful of my peers and role at the store. I told the two of them I kind of liked being "one of them" and I'm sure the scowl on my face while I said it killed any chance I had of landing the job.

For years that interview stayed engrained in my mind - it solidified my appreciation and respect for the work that happens on the shop floor. It also helped ground one of my core strengths in respect for the individual. I have long prided myself on treating associates at all levels of the organization with the same degree of respect and candor, whether they are on the shop floor or in the board room. Over my career and in the years since that job interview, I have seen many associates who have failed to grasp this simple concept. Those who take the view that corporate hierarchies and levels within an organization should drive how an associate gets treated are truly missing out. Respect for the individual is a core competency of leadership, and a trait that all who aspire to grow their career to the executive level must embrace. In light of the exchange at the job interview, and having had the benefit of twenty more years of experience since then, my thoughts on key learnings follow.

Listen to Understand

With years of hindsight and reflection, I am sure the intention of the hiring manager was not meant to disrespect my junior role or that of my peers. Had I probed him further I may have been able to extract that from him but given my inexperience in the corporate arena at that time I did not have the tools or the patience to do so. When you find yourself in a similar situation to that of the late adolescent described at the start of this chapter, think about how you would react. Given the chance to do it again and with the luxury of maturity and experience I did not have then I would have certainly asked a few more questions to gauge the intent of his comments. Listening is a skill that most of us need to work on, and one that I continue to focus on as a consultant deriving value and benefit for my clients.

Never Forget Your Roots

I am deeply satisfied with the time spent working on the shop floor and sincerely proud of the experiences and relationships built there. That is truly where the magic happens to bring the customer experience to life in most organizations. In my return to retail in 2010, I cherished the opportunity to spend time on the shop floor – be it working alongside DC associates on special projects, stocking shelves during the holidays, or reliving my early days as a produce associate during peak days. I learned more about the real issues at the company by working on the floor and engaging associates than I did with the 'experts' in the office. It was from shop floor engagement that some of our most prolific programs were launched, and some of my fondest memories were forged.

Respect Is a Two-Way Street

When I got my first corporate role at the industrial gas company, my coach and mentor told me you should always respect your employees, since you never know when you might be working for one of them. He would always add "you'll notice I am being exceptionally nice to you…". Good advice from a mentor and friend that still rings true today.

Further to the last point, that same hiring manager from decades ago referred to in the opening came to work in the same company as me in a role I had direct and deep dealings with. After spending hours with him engaging in the business at hand and implementing our strategy, I look back on our interaction many years ago and am confident his heart was in the right place when he made the comments about not being 'one of them anymore'. Spending time with him again makes me wonder what path my career could have taken if I had of taken the Pricing Manager role. In hindsight, I am thankful things have worked out the way they have, and mindful of the impact an interaction from twenty years ago can still have today.

Takeaways

For those that worked on the shop floor, you know there is no greater feeling than the ability to lead and engage a team that you can relate to. I still learn something new with every interaction and look back fondly on those years. I constantly tell my wife that when I retire from the executive ranks of the corporate and consulting world I will undoubtedly end up working on the shop floor somewhere to keep my passion alive. Whether you have spent your formative years there or not, you always have the opportunity to engage and seek counsel from your line associates. They are the last interaction you have with your customer and are the key to your company's reputation and financial results. Be respectful, always...

<u>20</u>

"Never Stop Improving"

The Graduation Story

In the spring of 1996 I achieved something nobody in my family had done before – I graduated from University. For me it was the culmination of years of effort and cerebral agony. While high school had been quite easy for me, University was not. The art of reading to understand, writing to convince, working and dissecting case studies to determine their practical implications were all very new concepts to me. With lots of hard work, I was able to attend convocation and bookend my time in London, Ontario.

During convocation at Western, we heard from Ted Rogers, founder and head of the iconic Canadian media company bearing his name. His speech was eloquent and inspiring. As I listened I thought here is someone who has worked exceptionally hard and received the lasting benefits associated with the effort put in. I walked out of the ceremony energized and ready to make my mark on the world.

When I returned home to the Greater Toronto Area I gleefully showed off my newly minted degree to my family. My siblings looked at it with little fanfare, and my dad uttered something that I still remember today. He looked at me and said "congratulations, now you have a $5 degree....just like everyone else." First off, those of you who have been to any form of post secondary education (or have kids that have) are painfully aware of the cost of higher education in this country. In my case, I had to pay my own way as my parents did not have the means to put me through school. I busted my hump in my summers and during the school year to cobble together enough money to eat and survive, let alone supplement the student loans I was lucky enough to obtain.

I did not harbour any ill feelings following that sly comment, quite the opposite actually. My dad was a straight shooter and "tell it like it is" guy - an immigrant from Northern Ireland, a plumber and boilermaker by profession. Like many middle-class families back in the day, he worked a day job in the city and did odd jobs and work on the side to pay the bills. Whether it was the day job, the odd jobs on the side, or the improvements in our own homes, he always seemed to have something going on.

What his counsel instilled in me was a hunger and drive to continue to improve my knowledge base and experience, not just in terms of education, but also in terms of practical life experience and skills. With respect to the latter, I have always prided myself on putting the skills he taught me as a youth into practice – from attending odd jobs with him and working as his 'unofficial apprentice', I was able to learn a great deal about plumbing, electrical and how to fix just about anything. On the education side, I was fortunate to apply my continued strive for excellence and obtain several accreditations and a Master's degree in the years that followed.

In recent years I have found myself mentoring many associates on the need to work hard to achieve exceptional results in their careers. One of the first things I counsel those who seek career advice on is the need to never stop improving. Whether it is seeking out specialized training or certification in your profession or formal education my advice to those who ask is to set your vision for where you want to be and plot your course to get there, using the means at your disposal to accomplish it. The advice I continue to pass on to mentees and associates is summarized here:

Plan Your Career

I've always been an advocate for planning your next move and how you will get there. It's only been in recent years that this process has been formalized with the help of several of my mentees. It was from those interactions The Personal Development One Pager was created. I speak about it often, one to one with my mentees and publicly at speaking events for professionals in multiple fields. In short, you need to map your career in terms of where you want to be in the future; articulate the skills, degrees and accreditations you have now and will need in future; and finally map out the actions you will take to get you where you need to go. Sounds easy? Try it then!

To download your FREE Personal Development One Pager Toolbox, visit the "Resources" tab at www.avleca.com and click on the link to download the tool including examples and instructions on how to use.

Never Stop Improving

The day you get that shiny new degree or certificate framed is the day you should be thinking about what's next. Is this latest achievement going to get you where you want to go longer term? If it is great – if not, start planning your next move. Most companies offer incentives and in some cases funding to increase your knowledge base or skillset. As you complete your 'Personal Development One Pager' and map out your development needs, talk to your human resources department about the resources available to you.

Build a Trusted Network of Advisors to Help You

If you are serious about wanting to improve your future, you need to surround yourself with people who truly want you to succeed in your goals. An advisory committee can be made up of friends, family, your coach at work or mentors you seek out. Whomever you enlist to join you on the journey, you need others to help guide you on the path to your chosen outcome.

Takeaways

While there are aspects of your personal and professional life that can enter various states of chaos over time, personal development of yourself and others is something that is completely in your control. It was almost a decade after my graduation from Western that I found myself walking across the auditorium stage at Queen's University in Kingston to collect my Master's Degree. This time was different from my earlier convocation in London – I had my dad, my wife, my infant daughter and my trusted advisory board all with me. When the ceremony was over and I regrouped with them I asked my dad if this one was worth $5. "No" he said, "this one is priceless…"

Think it, plan it, do it!

21

"Give Back"

The Volunteering Story

From 2007 to 2010 my family and I lived in Calgary, Alberta. It was an excellent city, with lots of things to do for kids and families. That time was also a very lucrative time for the oil and gas business – to the point where oil touched its peak price of almost $150 per barrel while we lived there.

A few months after moving to Calgary, I sought the opportunity to join the board of a not-for-profit organization. I had been on the board of a local transportation council in Ontario before I moved and wanted to continue that experience with another organization in Calgary. After a few months of searching, I was elected to the Board of Directors of the local chapter of the Boys and Girls Clubs. In the first few months I researched the organization and got to know the leadership team and fellow board members through our regular meetings.

What stuck out for me during my tenure was the unwavering commitment of the staff to the kids they helped and the resolve of the kids in their programs and care. For the last year I was there, we would conduct our board sessions at one of the properties in town, spending time before or after the session to engage with the staff and kids to better understand how we could help them as an organization. During those interactions, we heard harrowing tales of personal struggle, abuse and how thankful they were to have the support from the organization. Some of my fondest memories of being on the board are sitting down for a meal with the kids at the resident facilities. They would tell stories about their passions, their aspirations and what drives them. While these kids had all been through very challenging situations in their lives, I found it inspiring to hear them talk freely and openly about their drive for the future.

That time on the board was very moving for me. My entire life, I had been sheltered from the cruel reality that many kids face on a day to day basis. Spending time with them and sharing their experiences taught me a considerable amount about leadership. Some highlights for me follow.

Make the Most of the Situation

Regardless of the hand you've been dealt, you have the power to drive your future. In meeting the kids that we helped, it was truly inspiring to see them thrive with support from the community. Our annual meeting and celebration at the main office was an absolute gem – the ability to celebrate diversity of culture, the skills and passions they acquired and perhaps most importantly just seeing kids be kids. If a child who's been subject to harsh realities in life through no fault of their own can make the most of their situation do you think you could too?

You Can and Must Help Others

Many of us get so bogged down in our day to day lives that we lose sight of the need to help others. How can you help others when you have what seems like an endless array of your own challenges to address? Like other challenges in your work and personal life, you simply must take the time to give back. Your participation does not have to be with a large institution. Some start with one on one mentoring, joining church groups or other networking outlets. Others join professional organizations, boards of directors or industry working groups. Whatever it is that you land on, rest assured you will be helping yourself out in addition to those you attend with and for.

Helping Others Can Help You!

Helping others provides multiple benefits to the parties involved. The party on the receiving end gets access to your time, passion and expertise; and you get the satisfaction of knowing you are giving back to those in need. Helping others can help you more than you know, and can be the key to opening more doors for you in your personal and professional endeavours – some that you may not even know existed. How you may ask? The opportunity to join a not for profit board of directors can give you unapparelled access to other business leaders in the community, many of whom you may not have had the chance to engage with otherwise. Joining networking groups can help you meet people with like minded aspirations and in some cases, can help you land your next role. In addition, you get the opportunity to leverage the compounding effect of the contacts and relationships obtained. Each new contact you make is the opportunity for you to meet even more like minded associates – be sure you are willing to return the favour and watch your quality contacts multiply.

Takeaways

Getting out and helping others can seem like a daunting task when you have so much on the go already. The reality is that the key to being a successful leader and executive is built on a foundation of giving back to others. You must find a way to make the time to do so – besides, you never know when you or a loved one will be on the receiving end of that needed assistance. From sports teams to social services to networking to industry involvement, there are multiple ways you can get involved now to expand and drive your presence.

<u>22</u>

"Perception is Reality"
The Dispatching Story

As my career in logistics grew at the industrial gas company I was asked to take on more leadership duties, complementing my skills and presence in the company. My coach and mentor was a big proponent of pushing me beyond my comfort zone and into areas that would help me grow as an individual and future leader within the organization.

One such opportunity that I took great pride in was taking part in collective bargaining with the labour unions governing our driver Agreements. Since I had 'grown up' in logistics working as a dispatcher and worked my way into a management role, I had the luxury of knowing most of the drivers; including their individual needs, concerns and aspirations. Where possible, and while collective bargaining was underway, I would seize the opportunity to have one of my logistics planners dispatching on site from the driver terminal. In most cases, the locations were in Southern Ontario and close to the office so there was not much incremental travel or inconvenience to the staff to cover off the request. When we were negotiating in the Montreal region, we would have to get more creative in how we covered since that location was several hours from the head office.

During one of the negotiations in Montreal I was a part of I ended up splitting duties with my dispatch team and made sure I was present in the driver terminal and dispatching along side my team with the drivers. We were anticipating some concerns from the drivers about certain aspects of the contract, and I wanted to make sure that if there was a way I could leverage my relationship with the drivers to come up with a mutually satisfying Agreement I would make it happen. I enjoyed the opportunity to spend more time with the drivers, listening to and addressing their concerns real time when I could, helping to make sure that any minor disagreements or issues could be resolved prior to us meeting at the negotiating table. It also gave me the opportunity to practice conversing in French, something I did not get the chance to do much of anymore. When I was dispatching these same drivers earlier in my career I spent about 90% of my time speaking French, but was now only spending about 10% of my time speaking French due to the expanded, national aspect of my role.

The poignant moment in this story came on my second night in Montreal dispatching. I was on the phone with one of my team members in the Mississauga office after hours while I sat in the driver terminal at the planning workstation. We were talking about an issue he escalated and since he knew I was working in Montreal that night he just called me directly. When the issue was resolved and I hung up I noticed one of our seasonal drivers from the Gaspésie region of Quebec standing in the drivers room. He was in town to switch out a trailer for maintenance and was taking the opportunity to connect before heading back home. While we had only met in person once or twice, we had spoken on the phone hundreds of times over the years. He had a puzzled look on his face and I asked him what was wrong. He turned to me and said something I will never forget – "for a francophone you have the best English accent I have ever heard".

The irony in this story is he had never heard me speak English before. Since all our conversations had been in French, he just assumed that I was a Francophone and thought nothing of it. He was shocked when I broke the news to him that I was an Anglophone, learning my French in a grade school immersion program in Ontario. While I was flattered with the complement, it brought to light the powerful notion of perception being reality.

Perception is Reality

Transferring this experience to the broader business environment, how associates perceive you is your reality, whether you like it or not. I've seen numerous associates become flustered over the years with their inability to shake a stigma or past failure. The challenge is that while your actions and accomplishments define you personally, it is what people see and believe that drives how you are seen and understood by others. In many cases the reality thrust upon you by others is not fair, but like most things in business there is little you can do to change it, or is there?

Drive Your Reality

In the case of the driver from the Gaspésie, he had a positive perception that drove his reality of my lineage. While you may not be able to control how others perceive you, you do have the power to control what they see. Your body language, actions and accomplishments should always reflect the image you want to portray. If you have the ability to deliver like nobody else but can't lead a team or work with others you may be perceived to be difficult to work with and hence not able to produce. Similarly, I have seen instances where associates who had become masters of delegation and empowering others be accused of not doing anything. In both these cases, the associates could have changed the perception of them by driving the behaviours and actions they wanted noticed.

Takeaways

The lesson I learned that night is something all leaders should be aware of – how others perceive you is your reality! In the case of the driver who made the comment, we had known each other for years. Through our interactions and conversations over time, he envisioned a reality of who he thought I was. In this case, him finding out that French was my second language and an constant effort for me to speak helped grow our mutual respect even more than we already enjoyed. The same can not always be said for misplaced views on perception and your reality. Make sure you are conveying the leader you want others to see.

23

"Rally the Troops"

The Inventory Efficiency Story

In late 2012 I was asked to take on a corporate wide initiative on Inventory Efficiency for a large Canadian retailer, starting in the new year. At that time, there was pressure on the business to make a change, improve our inventory position and drive working capital. While I was disappointed to vacate my leadership role on the transportation team I had spent the past two years building and transforming, I knew in my heart it was the right decision for the business.

My first few days in role were interesting to say the least. The company had conducted an offsite meeting to brainstorm the various ways in which we as an organization would improve our inventory position. I was handed this information a few weeks after the meeting and committed to a target derived by the executives at the time. The target met the qualifications for a worthy goal; it was specific, measurable, achievable, realistic and timely. The challenge in all of it was the sheer size and scope of the initiative – we had to transform ways of working from one end of the company to the other, and fast. Early in 2013 the Inventory Efficiency Program was born!

While daunting at the outset, managing large projects and initiatives was not new for me. While at the industrial gas company, I ran their continuous improvement practice and led a team of dedicated Six Sigma Blackbelts and change agents. As I pulled the team together, we spent the first few weeks developing a project plan and trying to tackle the project steps we would undertake to drive results. By the end of the second month of the project, we had identified three main pillars of the program, defined key resources for each and developed a roadmap of how we would execute.

What happened in the coming weeks is a testament to the power of teamwork and what can happen when associates are driven and empowered to deliver results. Working with cross functional partners across the organization, we simultaneously implemented key ways of working and rules for how we 'Planned', 'Flowed' and 'Exited' product from the business. In addition, we leveraged top analytical resources to develop a clearly defined measurement system for what constituted productive and non-productive inventory in the business. All meetings in the company where inventory was discussed would now use this universally accepted measurement system to track performance and action plans. Where there had once been complexity and confusion surrounding our inventory position, we now had clarity like never before.

In the weeks that followed, there were varying rates of adoption by the stakeholders as they moved through the change curve. We had fundamentally changed how success was measured for multiple stakeholders in the business and not all had completely warmed up to the process. As the early adopters demonstrated that the new ways of working would improve their business, others followed suit. The executive team, while on board from the beginning, would now publicly celebrate and commend the associates for their efforts in improving inventory.

The culmination of our first six months of the Inventory Efficiency Program was a national clearance event held in the normally sleepy summer months before back to school marketing took off. We leveraged the partnership forged between the different organizations in the company to allow merchants to promote their clearance merchandise in the flyer over a three-week period. Store operators were brought into the program to facilitate execution well in advance. We collected every clearance sign we could find and aligned the store setup to delivery of the product, creating a friendly competition between stores on who could sell the most product. By the end of the three-week event, we had cleared tens of millions of dollars of inventory that would have otherwise been left to clog up our back rooms and distribution centres for years to come. That event, coupled with the Plan-Flow-Exit Rules and Ways of Working put into effect by the Inventory Efficiency Team and our cross functional partners would result in obtaining a world-class inventory result in just under two years.

As I said earlier in this chapter, I had managed several programs and initiatives over my career, even led entire continuous improvement teams and departments. This though was by far the biggest program I had led to date, and the most rewarding in terms of the cross functional collaboration and results driven for the company. While there were several factors that led to our success, not the least of which were the various change management methodologies and practices I have had the luxury of driving over the years, I would sum up our key success factors as follows.

Executive Involvement

While we inherited the target and the desired outcome for the program from the offsite held before we were formally handed the initiative, the executive leadership at the time had the foresight to give us the leeway we needed to drive success. Even though they were noticeably uneasy at times when we proposed changes to our measurement systems, processes and ways of working, they stuck with us and publicly drove the message hard about the need to succeed. When you are contemplating a large, cross functional initiative it is crucial to have the senior executives drive the program for you. If they are telling you they are supportive but downplaying it with others you may not be set up for success. In our case, we had complete alignment from post to post, helping us achieve even better results than we initially envisioned.

Standardized Measurement System

The development of the measurement system to track productive and non-productive inventory was as important as the executive presence identified above. In large companies, it is easy for complexity and complacency to rule. The development of a clear, concise tool to show which areas of the business were failing to meet their targets drove a level of engagement and sense of urgency not seen before in the business. We faced challenges to the validity of the data and categorization early on, not uncommon for change initiatives that are driving a new way of working. Knowing we had built a measurement system that could be validated using Six Sigma tools, we stuck to our guns and changed behaviour through the entire business for the benefit of not only our shareholders, but also our customers.

Be Persistent

Change is hard. Most corporate executives will tell you that getting a change initiative implemented can be compared to trying to turn a supertanker. It takes precision, patience and persistence to get it done right. In our case, we developed the Plan-Flow-Exit rules and Ways of Working cross functionally, held town hall and feed back sessions to gather and implement feedback, then drove the change. The laggards on the change curve resisted change at first, but were converted to believers when the groundswell of support from early adopters began to yield massive improvement for their businesses.

Takeaways

Throughout your career, you will be called on to rally the troops and drive a positive result for your organization. That may entail an initiative within your functional area, a corporate wide transformation or something in between. Whatever the case, you need to make sure you have the support, measurement systems and persistence to deliver. In my case, the success enjoyed and positive change created with the Inventory Efficiency Program gave me the confidence and passion to drive other transformational programs. You will find it is always possible to accomplish more as a team than you could ever do on your own.

24

"Be Aware"

The Airport Story

Over the years I have spent countless hours at the airport. Whether the travel has been domestic or somewhere abroad I have had the privilege of seeing many cities and by extension airports in my day. When travelling on a plane you never know who you might end up sitting beside. Unless you are travelling with someone and have had the seats around you assigned, most times you have no idea who the mysterious person is beside you.

This story is a two in one; both involving airports and both involving iconic Canadian musicians. The first happened during the early 2000's when I was doing lots of travelling in my merchant days with the industrial gas Company. The second was in July of 2008, when my dad was at the end of his battle with Cancer.

In the earlier encounter, I had landed back in Toronto and was waiting in line form my taxi outside the terminal when there was an altercation that caught my attention. The guy who was first in line, just in front of me, was cursing at a group of guys who were trying to in his words 'jump the line and take his cab'. They backed off when he protested and he proceeded to jump into the cab. As he rolled away in the taxi I turned to the guys beside me and said "what was his problem?".

I had not taken notice of them while standing there (face down in my smartphone) but when I lifted my head I instantly recognized who they were – the Canadian band Blue Rodeo. They answered that they had just got back from a long trip and charity hockey game as part of the Junos and were simply trying to get in the first cab they could acquire. We chatted for a few moments and when the next cab came they hopped in and were on their way. Had the guy in front of me not caused a stink I would never have even known they were there, nor would I have had the chance to chat with them.

The second story took place on a plane ride from Calgary to Toronto in July of 2008. My dad was deteriorating quickly, and I was commuting back and forth almost every week from Calgary to spend time with him before he passed. Though I did not know it, this trip would be the last before he passed away. At the time I was travelling so frequently I was able to buy flight passes and upgrade to first class. On this trip, I settled into my seat and proceeded to nap most of the way home. The trips back and forth, the concern about my dad, work and a young family were leaving me drained. When I woke up we were on our final decent into Toronto. As I came to and gathered myself I turned to the gentleman beside me and recognized him immediately - it was Tom Cochrane.

We chatted for a few minutes as the plane taxied and we collected our belongings. As we left the plane, I remarked to him that I would be singing his songs in my head for days following our encounter. He smiled and said "that's kind of the idea isn't it?". Indeed.

In both cases, I was pleasantly surprised at how down to earth these folks were. Personable, well spirited and humble all at once. I am sure they have had and continue to have multiple interactions with strangers and fans on an ongoing basis; the fact that they came across as ordinary Canadians when we met was intriguing to me. Those interactions taught me a few lessons about the need to understand what is going on around you and how to react.

Recognize Your Surroundings

You should make it a point to always know what is going on around you. Who is sitting beside you on that plane or standing beside you in line for a taxi at the airport? In my case I was completely oblivious in both instances, yielding a brief but memorable experience with each. As you relate this lesson to the business world, you must always be aware of what is going on around you. Are the ideas and initiatives you are working on still relevant? Will you be subject to changes and challenges in the coming days? These are areas where you need to make sure you can observe and interpret what is happening around you and what the implications are.

Think Before You Act

In the case of the guy in line for a taxi who cursed out the road-weary band on their way home, he likely had no idea who he was talking to and had no way of obtaining feedback on his actions. Before we knew it, he was in the cab and gone. Think about your own situation – how many times have you blurted something out in a meeting or with a co-worker that you wish you could have stated differently? Perhaps the words did not come out right or your comment was made at a completely inopportune time. Either way, you must make sure to take the time to think about what you will say or do before you actually do it. Once you say the words or take the action, it is very hard to undo the damage you may create.

Takeaways

Like Chapter 16 'You Never Know', this chapter provides a couple of simple examples of the power of understanding your surroundings. You can control your interactions with others and how you come across. Are you the type of person who pushes forward with no consideration about what is going on around you, or are you the type of person who can take a step back to reflect, recognize their surroundings and act accordingly?

<u>25</u>

"Love Life"

The Hospital Story

'Staring at the ceiling' – the first line in the Introduction of this book and a true statement with respect to its development. What I did not convey in the opening was where or the reason why. Turns out the concept for this book and the 'Reflections' on my social media feeds that came before it was actually the result of staring at the ceiling in the hospital for almost a week.

Throughout my life I have prided myself on being active and healthy. Throughout the book you have seen examples of my love of sport and staying active with my wife and kids. My trip to the hospital in February 2016 actually started out as a pretty ordinary day for me. I had been to the gym, to the office and was just arriving home after a night of public skating with my daughters at the local arena.

When we arrived home my wife and I began prepping the kids for bed, our nightly routine. I went down to the basement office briefly to drop my work bag off and get some things organized for the next day as I did most nights. While I was down there I felt a sharp pain in my abdominal area. It began to intensify and I started feeling nauseous and light headed. I pulled myself up the stairs and flopped down on the couch in the family room. I called out to my wife who was still upstairs with the kids and told her something was wrong – she needed to call 911 for help.

After receiving a diagnosis, I was very thankful to know I would be okay and that the condition was common and manageable. For the first time in a long time, I had the opportunity to rest for a few days. Up to that point I had been going non-stop - work, sports, houses, cottages and family had occupied most of my time. It was during my few days in hospital that I realized how thankful I am to have had the experiences I've had in my life. With further pause and reflection I decided I needed to put pen to paper and bring them to a broader audience, hence the social media blogs and this book.

Most important of all in those days at the hospital and the time since has been a complete and renewed faith in my family, my life's work and my surroundings. If I feel like I am in the midst of a tough situation, I need only think back to the scare in February to realize just how lucky I am to be here today. Some reflections from 'staring at the ceiling' time in hospital follow.

Love Your Life

Every day above ground is a good day and should be embraced. I am thankful for the interactions I have with colleagues, clients, friends and family. While I have enjoyed a vibrant and playful sense of humour over the years, it is amplified now to the point where I truly appreciate all that is around me. A setback or challenge in life that would have occupied my thought space in the past is no longer given much if any consideration. All energy and effort is spent enjoying the moment and looking forward to what's next.

Love Your Work

Most of the chapters and stories in this book are about work. I have reveled in being a passionate and driven corporate employee and executive. Just prior to being admitted to hospital, I started my company, The Avleca Group Inc. knowing that I wanted to bring my experience, passion and knowledge to a much broader customer base. While I am truly grateful for the experiences, friends and contacts built in the corporate world, I have no regrets about venturing out on my own. Working for myself has only served to amplify the passion and commitment I bring to my clients.

Takeaways

Above all else, remember that you are in control of your life. While you may not have complete control of your health, you can control how you react to the hand you've been dealt. Take the time to enjoy your friends, family, loved ones and even your work.

Thank you for taking the time to read this, I hope you have enjoyed these reflections and garnered some useful tools you can use in your own career. I wish you the best of luck in all you do…

Craving more? Visit www.avleca.com for FREE insights and material on how to drive your career.